*Interdisciplinary Studies on
Family, Kinship, and Marriage*

WORKING TOGETHER:
WOMEN AND FAMILY IN SOUTHWESTERN SASKATCHEWAN

*Interdisciplinary Studies on
Family, Kinship, and Marriage
General Editor: K. Ishwaran*

WORKING TOGETHER: WOMEN AND FAMILY IN SOUTHWESTERN SASKATCHEWAN

Seena B. Kohl

Holt, Rinehart and Winston of Canada, Limited
Toronto   Montreal

Copyright © 1976
Holt, Rinehart and Winston of Canada, Limited
Toronto   Montreal

ISBN 0-03-923369-3
Library of Congress Catalog Card No. 75-1631
All Rights Reserved

It is illegal to reproduce any portion of this book except by special arrangement with the publishers. Reproduction of this material without authorization by any duplication process whatsoever is a violation of copyright.

Printed in U.S.A.
1 2 3 4 5   80 79 78 77 76

Foreword

About the Author
Seena B. Kohl is Associate Professor of Anthropology at Webster College, St. Louis, Missouri. She received her B.A. from San Francisco State College, San Francisco, and her M.A. and Ph.D. from Washington University, St. Louis. She received a post-Doctoral award and participated in a summer seminar in Southeast Asia (Indonesia and Singapore) under the auspices of the Department of the East Asian Language and Area Center, Washington University. From 1963 onwards Dr Kohl was involved in the Saskatchewan Cultural Ecology Research Project directed by Professor John Bennett. This book, as well as her previous publications, has been based on this research.

About the Book
The present monograph is part of a more comprehensive study of the Jasper region by a group of scholars, each focusing on a selected aspect of the agricultural family and its role in North American rural life. But it also has wider implications for understanding similar communities elsewhere.

Dr Kohl's work is set within the framework of family sociology with a special emphasis on the strategic role of women in the interdependent systems of the household and the agricultural enterprise in the rural Jasper region in the southwestern part of Saskatchewan. Within this rural system, the author makes a further differentiation between ranching and farming as life-styles.

Though this is a technical work, the author has also tried to accommodate two kinds of nonspecialist readers: the general readers desiring to know about other people, and the people studied – the Jasper folk – in the hope that self-knowledge may lead to a better life. Accordingly, the style of writing is a blend of vivid narrative and sharp empirical analysis.

The author, who cites Dell Hymes approvingly in her Preface, identifies her work with the new movement in anthropology which seeks to share its knowledge with the community studied. She, therefore, attempts to maintain a balance between practical concern and scientific objectivity.

Methodologically, the present study is somewhat eclectic, drawing on techniques from anthropology, sociology, history, and economics. In fact, in a methodological appendix, the author rightly questions the utility of the sociology-anthropology distinction in the study of human groups, no matter where such groups belong or at what stage of development they find themselves.

In its substantive content, this volume examines the structured conflicts and tensions that are generated in an agrarian community, especially the tensions between father and son over the command of the family enterprise. Equally significant for an understanding of the Jasper people is her analysis of the dual and strategic role of women as they become involved simultaneously in household and economic functions. Dr Kohl uses considerable skill in identifying and analyzing patterns of feminine social behaviour, and then in developing a typology of housewives. On the basis of carefully recorded case studies, she is able to place within such a typology women who are ideologically committed to a rural life-style and women who are, for personal situational reasons, anxious to get away from the rural life. Contrary to the sociological conventional images of feminine conservatism in rural society, Dr Kohl finds the women to be the least conservative component of the Jasper rural family. They seem to be the ones who have a broader background, are better educated, and are generally outward-looking.

Dr Kohl certainly uses the structuralist-functionalist approach in her study of roles, but she also goes well beyond it to offer a more situationally-oriented analysis. This means that, instead of clamping a preconceived structure on the people studied, she allows the structures of their relationships to emerge logically through a detailed presentation of firsthand, authentic experience in the language of the people themselves.

A special mention must be made of Professor John W. Bennett's scholarly intervention at the end of Dr Kohl's study. His Supplementary Essay on Hutterite Women provides comparative data on a neighbouring group which is more closed, more ideologically committed, and yet quite adaptive to change. This essay indicates both points of similarity and dissimilarity between the role of women in the two communities. The similarities stem from a common agricultural background, while the differences arise from ideological and cultural dissimilarities. Professor Bennett notes the contradictions and tensions that arise in a community that combines an early Christian egalitarianism with the Biblical authoritarian principle of male dominance. He also shows how Hutterite society manages to overcome these problems through the mechanism of cultural and ideological socialization. The Supplement is a significant contribution to an understanding of Jasper rural folk in a comparative perspective.

K. Ishwaran
General Editor
York University

Preface

This book is one of several published contributions to the study of a rural region in southwestern Saskatchewan conducted by John W. Bennett and associates over a decade in the nineteen-sixties and seventies. The research was supported by grants from the National Science Foundation, the National Institute of Mental Health, the Agricultural Development Council, the Wenner-Gren Foundation, and Washington University (St. Louis, Missouri).

The present volume focuses on the data acquired by the writer as the researcher charged with the study of family and kinship. Bennett was primarily concerned with the ecology, economics, and decision-making operations of agricultural enterprises and the town communities. He also did studies of Hutterian Brethren colonies in the region, and has contributed a comparative chapter on Hutterian women to this volume.

The major theme of the research came to centre on the agricultural family and its properties: the mingling of kinship and economic functions which constitute the essential basis of rural life both in North America and the rest of the world. For the economic and background details which underlie this treatment of social relations, the reader should refer to J.W. Bennett, *Northern Plainsmen,* rev. ed. (Chicago: Aldine Publishing Company, 1971). A more specialized book-length study of agricultural management and ecology is in preparation.

This volume is primarily concerned with the interaction between the agricultural enterprise and the household, and the pivotal position the woman holds in both spheres. Given this focus, there are a number of topics which, although referred to, are not discussed, for example, schools and schooling, churches and clubs, rituals and ceremonies.

Working Together has been written primarily for the student and general audience, although some of its findings will have particular interest for those engaged in the analysis of women's work and relationships. However, it is hoped that the detailing of the work of women in the economic enterprise and their position in the family household will prove particularly useful to those same women. Dell Hymes writes:

> ... An essential part of ethnography is to learn, and formulate, what others already in a sense know. Heretofore, the ethnographer has mediated between such specific knowledge and general knowledge usually entirely in the direction of the latter, as represented in a professional community and publications. As far as possible, the mediation must go also the other way — even primarily the other

way. By helping members of a community to comprehend social reality more explicitly and generally, one may help people to employ what C. Wright Mills called "sociological imagination"... and to be in greater rational control of their own destinies.[1]

This book is for the women of Jasper.

Particular acknowledgements are due to Geri Binion and Terry Yokota, each of whom played a special role in helping to translate the research data into print. The writer is indebted to Charles Thomas for sharing his field materials. A special debt of gratitude is owed to Mildred Gilchrist and Mary Hanson and, above all, to John Bennett and Dan Kohl, without whose aid this book could not have been written.

Seena B. Kohl
Webster College

---

[1] Dell Hymes, "The Use of Anthropology: Critical, Political, Personal," in Dell Hymes, ed., *Reinventing Anthropology* (New York: Random House, 1969), pp. 53-54.

Contents

FOREWORD vii

PREFACE ix

INTRODUCTION 1
Family, Household, and Enterprise: Some Distinctions 3

CHAPTER I: THE JASPER REGION: SOCIAL GEOGRAPHY 8
The Plains: A Geographical Survey 8
The Jasper Region 9
   Population Centres 13

CHAPTER II: RESOURCES, CONSUMPTION, AND REPUTATION 16
Social Esteem or Reputation 19
Power 21

CHAPTER III: THE MAKING OF A SOCIAL COMMUNITY: THE ROLE OF WOMEN 24
Settlement Phase I: Pre-Homestead Cattlemen 25
Settlement Phase II: Homestead Farm 28
The Frontier Experience 30
Women on the Frontier 32

CHAPTER IV: COMMUNICATION NETWORKS AND SOCIAL CONTROL 37
Kinship Connections 38
Formal Organizations 40
Ties of Friendship 42
Economic Exchange 42
Processes of Communication 43
Social Control 46

CHAPTER V: THE INDIVIDUAL LIFE CYCLE: A PARTICIPANT IN THE FAMILY ENTERPRISE 52
Infancy and Childhood 53

Adolescence and Young Adulthood 54
Daughters and Sons 56
Adulthood 59
Aging 64

CHAPTER VI: FAMILY ROLES AND RELATIONSHIPS 66

Husbands and Wives 67
Parents and Children 72
Issues of Authority and Generation: Decorum 72
Issues of Authority and Generation: Sanctions 74
Work and Responsibility: The View of Childhood 75
Parents, Children, and Maturity 78
   Fathers and Sons 78
   Mothers and Daughters 84
   Grandparents, Parents, and Grandchildren 87
   Siblings 88
The Wider Kin Group 90

CHAPTER VII: WOMEN AND THE FAMILY ENTERPRISE 92

Women's Participation in the Enterprise 94
The Wife as Active Participant in the Family Enterprise 95
The Ambivalent Farm Housewife 96
The Participating Ranch Wife 100
The Contented Non-Participant 103
The Woman Who Wants Out 105
The Woman as Enterprise Operator 106
Summary 107

SUPPLEMENTARY ESSAY: A COMPARISON: HUTTERITE WOMEN AND THEIR FAMILIES, by John W. Bennett 109

The Life Cycle: Childhood 113
The Life Cycle: Marriage and Adulthood 116
Role Dualism 120
Change and Transition 122

APPENDIX: METHODS OF RESEARCH 126

BIBLIOGRAPHY 133

Interdisciplinary Studies on
Family, Kinship, and Marriage

Introduction

This book is about families who live on widely dispersed farmsteads in the southwestern section of Saskatchewan. It is as much about women as it is about family, since it is impossible to look at one without considering the other. Nor can the situation of women be understood without relating it to the larger social system in which they are embedded.

The locale of the study is loosely defined as the Jasper[1] region, an area of approximately four thousand square miles. Jasper town, with a population of some 2500 persons, is the site of the region's hospital, consolidated high school, major banks and post office, and principal religious and fraternal groups. The total population of the region, as we have defined it, is about nine thousand persons.[2]

The sample population on which this study is based consists of some four hundred persons comprising about one hundred and seventy households. We did not "sample" the town population, although we in-

---

[1] "Jasper", the names of other towns, neighbourhoods, and individuals are all pseudonyms, and not to be confused with Jasper, Alberta, Canada.
[2] Actual Census of Canada figures are: 1961, 9912 persons; 1971, 8560 persons.

terviewed extensively in the towns. The livelihood of the families consists in the production and sale of cattle and grain. Despite their geographic isolation, these families are fully functioning members of the Canadian socio-economic scene.

Settlement of the Jasper region is relatively recent. The earliest settlers — cattlemen — arrived in the 1880s, and the year 1906 witnessed the end of the open range. Districts were established for homesteading around 1900, with the majority of farm homesteaders arriving during the years 1912 through 1916. Common to much of prairie settlement, the initial optimism of the homesteaders was not matched by the economic potential of the initial 160-acre agricultural enterprise which homestead laws made possible. This led to considerable population turnover and decline before any degree of social and economic stability was achieved.

The standard 160-acre settlement unit could be owned outright after three years' residence, the making of "improvements" (a house and the breaking of sod), and the payment of a ten-dollar registration fee. Although regulations changed during the homestead period, there was generally an option to purchase an additional one-quarter section, called a "pre-emption", usually adjoining the homestead quarter. The cost was three dollars an acre, one-third to be paid within the first three years, the balance to be paid in five equal annual payments.

The basic conception which guided this land policy was that of the self-contained agricultural enterprise, which assumes that all necessary resources be available within the area of its own tenured land. This system, while expedient for lands administration, was unsuitable for maintenance of agriculture on semi-arid plains. The amount of 160 acres, which seemed so large to those from the east, was not sufficient for the plains. There were huge gaps between the expectation of fulfilling one's homestead claim and the reality of securing title. Over 40 percent of the homesteads were never "proved up", and four out of every ten Canadian homesteaders failed to secure title to their claim.[3]

The agricultural families of the period of study, 1962-1972, are the children and grandchildren of the initial homestead population, and Jasperites are fully aware of the hardships of these settlers. The struggles of the prior generation during the homestead-pioneer period and during the drought and depression of the 1930s were both recent enough and sufficiently vivid to influence the behaviour and aspirations of the contemporary Jasper population. Continuity of family enterprise is a major goal around which most families organize their expectations.

The region is part of the northern Great Plains and, like all midcontinental regions, is subject to sudden storms and great variation in

---

[3] Vernon C. Fowke, *The National Policy and the Wheat Economy* (Toronto: University of Toronto Press, 1957), p. 286.

temperature and rainfall. The variability and uncertainty of climate, particularly rainfall, creates special hazards for the agriculturalist and makes the area a high-risk economic environment. During the sixty years of settlement, various social and technological innovations have served to mitigate some of the risks. Within the region there are areas with significantly varying resources, and the use and development of these form the bases for the processes of social life.

This analysis of women and family life is based on data recorded as part of a larger project whose goal was to examine the cultural ecology of a modern North American agrarian population.[4] Research began in 1962 with two periods of intensive field work during 1963 and 1964, and again in 1970 and 1971. However, throughout the decade, contact was maintained through short visits to the region, correspondence, and the regional newspaper. Although the research project was not originally conceived as a longitudinal study, it became one, and the time span allowed the recording of the coming of age of one part of the population and an analysis of key factors emerging in different phases of the family cycle.

The overall frame of reference of the larger project has emphasized the concept of strategic action. In this frame of reference, the observer focuses on those strategies or coping mechanisms (both acts and nonacts) that men and women use in an attempt to exert control over their environment, both social and natural, in order to realize their own goals. The conceptualization of human behaviour in these terms directs attention to the individual choices which are made within an existing structure of alternatives. These are choices which have social as well as individual significance, the consequences of which can be analyzed in terms of enterprise maintenance and development and in terms of family roles and relationships. The present work focuses on the latter aspect.

Family, Household, and Enterprise: Some Distinctions

For conceptual clarity it is desirable to separate family, household, and enterprise. By *family* we mean those individuals who are linked to one another through ties of marriage or descent: kinsmen. The recognition of these linkages is variable, but nevertheless the according of "family" membership implies a special connection, distinct from ties of friendship or association or neighbourhood. It is necessary to distinguish the family from the residential group, or what we have called the

---

[4] See John W. Bennett, *Northern Plainsmen: Adaptive Strategy and Agrarian Life* (Chicago: Aldine Press, 1969-71), for a review of the research as a whole.

household. By household we mean a residential unit with independent cooking facilities. For the most part agricultural households in Jasper are composed of parents and their unmarried children (see Table 8, Chapter VI). We use the term *family household* to emphasize that households are units of kinsmen.

The *enterprise* is the agricultural production unit — the family farm or ranch. The enterprise can include more than one family household (see Table 9, Chapter VI); however, just as family households are for the most part composed of parents and their unmarried children, parents and their children comprise the agricultural enterprise as well. Thus the household and enterprise are most commonly composed of the same individuals but there are different goals. The agricultural enterprise goals are concerned with production; the family household is concerned with the maintenance and care of the household members. Each is dependent upon the other.

Many aspects of Jasper family life will be familiar to most North American readers. As compared with urban families, what is unique is the fact that Jasper families cannot be considered apart from the agricultural enterprise. The family agricultural enterprise — the "family farm" — is an unusual institution in North America, since in these enterprises there is no separation of economic and social roles. This is apparent when one recognizes that in the family farm the individual proprietor is simultaneously owner, manager, labourer and also father, husband, son; or, when one realizes that marriage partners are also business partners — either *de jure* or *de facto.*

These roles, with their varying and sometimes contradictory set of expectations for behaviour, are all played out within the boundaries of the farmstead. While this type of merged role behaviour is routine for agricultural societies throughout the world, in North America — where lives are most often distinctly divided into work and nonwork segments — there are important consequences for family household members. Of particular interest is the unique position of the rural woman who, unlike her urban sister, is intimately connected to the public extradomestic sphere of the male[5] because this public sphere is at the same time the domestic sphere, the family household being inextricably linked to the agricultural enterprise. The integration of the woman's domestic sphere of the household with the public sphere of the agricultural enterprise in effect creates a social situation where women do

---

[5] The distinction between public and private spheres — the male and female arenas — follows other analyses of women's roles which have explored the separation of man's work in social production and woman's work in the household, relating these differences in productive responsibility to the more politically-dominant position of men in all societies. See Michelle Zimbalist Rosaldo, "Women, Culture and Society: A Theoretical Overview," in M. Z. Rosaldo and L. Lamphere, eds., *Women, Culture and Society* (Stanford, California: Stanford University Press, 1974), pp. 1-42.

become active participants in what is defined ideologically as the man's world, but not *vice versa*. One consequence is that women have alternatives for gender roles. They may choose to play an active role in the operation of the enterprise or may restrict their attention to the household. (The possibility of women playing an active economic role has not evolved to the point of daughters being considered potential successors.)[6] Men, on the other hand, play only the one, traditional role, that of proprietor of the enterprise.

The position of the rural young man is defined by the fact that entrance into an agricultural occupation is made through an extended apprenticeship of the son to the father such that the operator is required to be father/boss to his son/hired hand. Apprenticeship of the son to the father begins early in life, but it is during the son's adolescence and early adulthood that strains and tensions within the family household are most apparent. High value is placed upon the young person demonstrating both social and economic independence by the time he or she is twenty years old. However, apprenticeship and entrance into agriculture demand dependence upon the family economic unit. During this period the son generally attempts to establish an independent role, but if he desires to take over the enterprise he is constrained to remain within the family enterprise and under his father's tutelage.

The family agricultural enterprise is based upon the availability of labour within the residential group – the domestic household – which ideally,[7] as well as most commonly, consists of members of the nuclear family: father, mother, offspring. As a consequence, the labour resources for the enterprise are limited and depend upon the phase in the domestic cycle.[8] Obviously, small children do not contribute to the success of the enterprise, but older children do. The relationship between the domestic cycle and the needs of the enterprise are in constant tension, involving allocation of time and economic resources. This tension – which must be continually coped with – is not only affected by household composition and the ages and number of children, factors which directly affect the issue of labour availability, but also the physical health of household members and psychosocial factors. The latter involve the way in which the "need" for help is viewed and the way family household members preferentially allocate their time and labour.

---

[6] Daughters are active participants in the enterprise activities, and they *do* inherit property. Some women are enterprise heads, but only by default. This is discussed further in Chapter IV.

[7] The small family farm is often presented as a cherished form of institutional life, and this view has been the basis for many governmental policies, both in the United States and in Canada. See J. C. Gibson, *Family Farm Business Arrangements, Agricultural Economics, Bulletin 1* (University of Manitoba, 1959); Whitney Griswold, *Farming and Democracy* (New York: Harcourt, Brace and Company, 1948); and Harold Breimeyer, *Individual Freedom and the Economic Organization of Agriculture* (Urbana: University of Illinois Press, 1965).

[8] The span of the family cycle has been divided into different numbers of stages by different writers, although all agree on a minimum of stages: the married couple without

It is within the domestic sphere that the woman becomes of critical importance in setting the style of consumption and level of activity for her participation and that of the other household members in the enterprise. Emphasis in this study has been placed on examining the role of women in both generating and resolving the conflicts or the potential conflicts between the demands placed on the shared resources of family household and enterprise.

Not only does the phase of the developmental cycle of the domestic group determine the constraints with which the operator/father must cope, but the development phase of the enterprise[9] sets constraints upon the household. The establishment process of an enterprise requires deferment of consumption wants, and members of the household must be willing to make the necessary sacrifices. Throughout all phases of enterprise development there is a constant juggling of family and enterprise needs. At the same time, external factors such as the price of wheat, the availability of credit, or the vagaries of the weather establish a set of external constraints which must be taken into consideration in the operation of the enterprise. There are styles of strategic responses (recognized both by Jasper agriculturalists as well as the observers) which emphasize enterprise development over family household wants, while other styles value individual developmental desires over those choices which would allocate resources to the development of the enterprise. These strategic styles are important in the delineating of alternative family life styles among Jasperites.

All families must deal with the biosocial issues of age and sex, family rights and obligations, and autonomy and power; furthermore, all families evolve their own cultural rules or styles of interaction which enable them to accomplish their day-to-day tasks. Expectations are set and a behaviour routine within the family group evolves over time so that it is possible to abstract from the style of interaction between the members what Hess and Handel have called "family themes".[10] This is

---

children, the couple with preschool children only, the family with school-age children, the couple with no children left at home, and the widow or widower. See F. Ivan Nye and Felix M. Berardo, *The Family: Its Structure and Interaction* (New York: The MacMillan Company, 1973), p. 23.

[9] Developmental phases of the enterprise are defined by the researchers and Jasperites as follows:
    1. Establishment, what Jasper calls "starting out" or the beginning of establishing an independent enterprise.
    2. Development, the expansion and intensification of resources.
    3. Maintaining, the period in which a plateau of development has been reached.
    4. Transmission, the period of the transfer of resources.

[10] Robert Hess and Gerald Handel, *Family Worlds* (Chicago: University of Chicago Press, 1959), pp. 11-13.

similar to Oscar Lewis' phrase, the "culture of the family".[11] These are the patterns of behaviour and the shared agreements which differentiate one domestic group from another. However, although each family household is unique, each household also shares with others similar understandings and styles of interaction. In particular, we find that the similar work demands set by the agricultural enterprise upon family household members, regardless of their personal proclivities, establish a situation in which there is wide agreement and consensus as to family expectations and behaviour with regard to age and sex within the region.

The first two chapters of the book survey the geography and society of the region. Chapter III reviews the historical development of the region with particular attention paid to the role of women in establishing a social community. Chapter IV presents the contemporary Jasper social system. Chapter V deals with the individual life cycle, or growing up in a household which is also an economic enterprise. Chapter VI examines the role expectations for household members: husbands and wives, parents and children, siblings and other kinsmen. Chapter VII discusses the role of the woman in the enterprise. Lastly, in a supplementary essay to the work, John Bennett has provided a comparative essay which contrasts the position of Hutterite women with that of Jasper women. The methods of research are discussed in an appendix.

---

[11] Oscar Lewis, "An Anthropological Approach to Family Studies," *American Journal of Sociology*, 55(1950), 468-475.

CHAPTER I

The Jasper Region: Social Geography

The Plains: A Geographical Survey

The Jasper region, as we define it, is a 4700-square-mile rectangle in the southwestern corner of the province of Saskatchewan, the central of the three Prairie Provinces of west-central Canada. The Plains landscape is one of rolling grassland — empty or spacious, depending upon one's frame of reference. The great open sky and the long horizons become important symbols for Jasperites when they compare the region with other places:

> It's the sky I missed when I went back east...
> the trees get in the way and you can't see it...

Wallace Stegner, the American novelist, who spent a few years of his childhood in the Jasper region, describes it in a more literary fashion:

> The drama of this landscape is in the sky, pouring with light and always moving. The earth is passive. And yet the beauty I am

struck by, both as present fact and as revived memory, is a fusion: this sky would not be so spectacular without this earth to change and glow and darken under it ... The very scale, the hugeness of simple forms, emphasizes stability ... These prairies are quiescent, close to static; looked at for any length of time, they begin to impose their awful perfection on the observer's mind. Eternity is a peneplain.[1]

Highly variable climactic conditions are typical of this area: severe winters, hot summers, variable frost-free growing seasons depending on altitude, periodic droughts, and severe wind and hail storms. It is the variability of rainfall which is most crucial for agricultural production, and water is the dominant climactic resource of the Plains around which agricultural life is focused.[2]

The low relief and treelessness of the Plains also encourages the formation of strong winds which are most severe in the spring and fall and cause soil-blowing with little protection for the sandy, light soils. While the Canadian Plains are deficient in moisture, marginal in temperature, and very windy – all of these creating difficulties for crop agriculture – , the high latitude provides an extended period of daylight, especially during the growing season, which makes possible the rapid growth of grain crops.

The Jasper Region

The Jasper region is located at the western edge of the driest part of the northern Great Plains grain-livestock area. Within the region there are three major topographic divisions: plains to the north and south divided centrally by a range of forested hills containing a provincial park (see Map I). These are the Cypress Hills, a 4200-foot elevation containing Rocky Mountain flora and fauna. The presence of the Cypress Hills provides a source of run-off snow and modifies the aridity, climate, and vegetation of the region, permitting a greater variety of economic adaptation.

The plains, the hills, and the underlying glacial till and soils constitute a remarkably varied resource constellation for agriculture. There are four principal subregions with differing economic implications: the plateau of the Cypress Hills (4200-4000 ft.); the slopes of the Hills (4000-3000 ft.), extending from the plateau area to the two plains levels (3000-2400 ft). These latter have flat to rolling topography.

---

[1] Wallace Stegner, *Wolf Willow* (New York: The Viking Press, 1955), p. 7.
[2] An urban visitor to the region immediately notices the way in which rainfall is a dominant topic of conversation even at the level of four-year-olds. One of our earliest field notes is that of a conversation held with a four-year-old who discussed the fact that it rained last week, but not this week, and whether it was going to rain next week!

The Jasper Region viewed from the crest of the Cypress Hills.

A Typical Jasper Region small town main street.

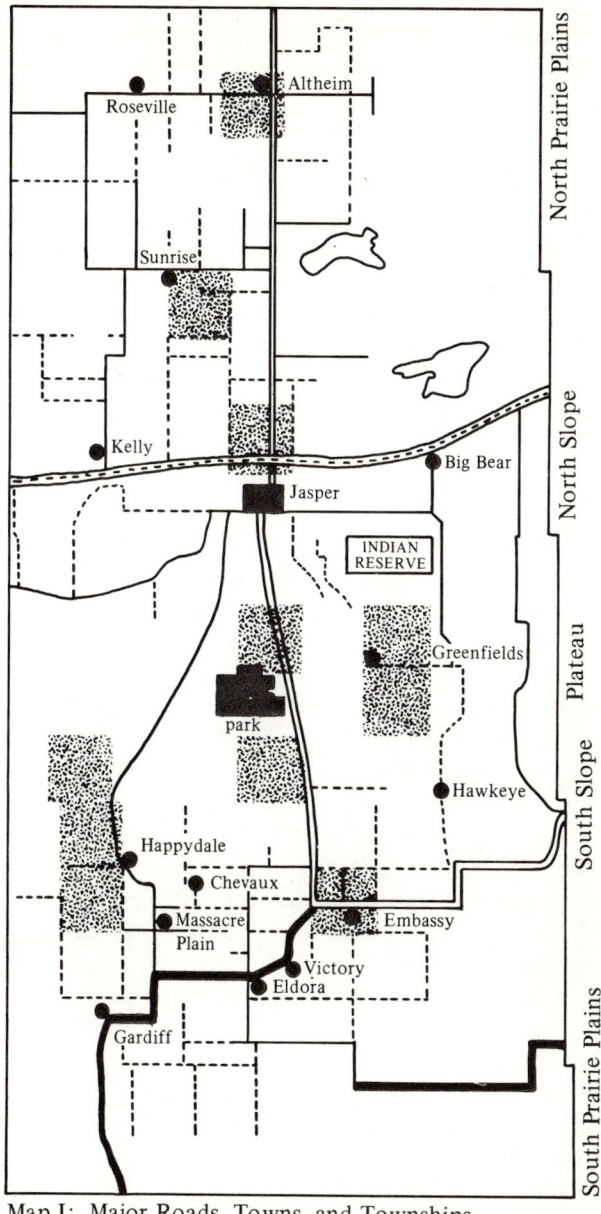

Map I: Major Roads, Towns, and Townships.

======== Transcontinental Highway
═══ Paved Highway
▬▬▬ Good Gravel Road
------ Unimproved Road, Impassable in bad weather
▓▓▓ Specimen Townships

The initial settlement of the region in the 1880s and 1890s established a ranching economy throughout the area. Sites in the hills were used for summer pasture and the cattle were turned loose on the prairies during the winter. Homesteading beginning in the eighteen-nineties – but not significant until 1910 onwards – reserved the plains for farming. Most ranch homesteads were located on the slopes, usually in protected sites in the "coulees", or stream canyons. The contemporary period has seen the emergence of an intensive cattle-raising regime by farmers on the plains resulting from the need to supplement the income received from grain. In general, the contemporary ranching population resides on the slopes and the plateau, and the contemporary farming population is concentrated on the prairies. There is overlap in only a very few locations.

The region is sparsely populated – about 1.7 persons per square mile. In the hills, where ranching is the dominant agricultural activity, the population density is even less – about one person per square mile. Often the ranch homestead is located between one to seven miles from the main road. Farm houses in the more heavily homesteaded plains were situated with easy access to the road, although access to village service centres has remained an important social issue.

In 1963 there was one major all-weather north-south road which led from the Trans-Canada Highway to the Cypress Hills Park; the other roads were gravel and dirt and required constant maintenance by the road crew. Travel south from the Cypress Hills Park to the United States border was via a poor gravel road. In rain or snow, travel anywhere in the region was quite hazardous. For the most part, local traffic passed through the town of Jasper and then north five miles to the Trans-Canada Highway. By 1970 the major north-south highway was completely paved, as was the southern road which crossed the lower portion of the region connecting the small towns of Embassy and Eldora. Nevertheless, many of the outlying districts still faced hazardous travel conditions during winter and after severe rainstorms, and construction of passable all-weather roads throughout the region remained a problem (see Map I).

Since settlement of the region was late and economic stabilization of agricultural enterprises recent, the accepted conveniences of urban life were late in entering the region. The electrification of rural areas in Saskatchewan was accomplished by 1956, and in 1962 (at the beginning of the research project) every house, except one, in our study population had electricity. Other amenities – plumbing, phones, and passable roads – were still in the process of entering the region and were not widely available in the more isolated districts. As a consequence, although a house may have had electricity and certain electrical appliances (particularly a freezer), running water or indoor plumbing may have been absent. By the end of the decade of our research, the house without indoor plumbing and running water was rare and telephone service to the more isolated districts was common.

Population Centres

The town of Jasper was the first town settlement in the region. It was founded in 1883 as a camp for Canadian Pacific Railroad labourers, and incorporated in 1903. Through this railhead entered nearly all of the people who settled the rectangle which forms the boundaries of the Jasper region as we define it. The branch line of the railroad (and the associated villages which sprang up along its track) across the southern half of the region was not established until 1915, after the intensive farming settlement had begun. With the decline in population, many of these small villages, once thriving population centres during the height of homesteading, have virtually vanished (see Table 1).

Contrasted with the remaining small villages in the region, Jasper represents a functioning social community. In addition to the regional facilities (such as the hospital, consolidated high school, retirement home, and provincial offices), there was a small business district some four blocks in length along which were located the cafés (3), clothing stores (4), banks (2), post office, hotels (2), theatre, and grocery stores (2). Jasper also boasted completely paved streets (all accomplished in the summer of 1964), a municipal swimming pool, skating rink, and a regional museum as well as other service facilities (laundry, drugstore, hardware, and so on). In addition, the town businessmen have self-consciously celebrated the rancher as pioneer and culture hero. Jasper calls itself the "Old Cow Town"; its annual rodeo is an important element in the maintenance of the cowboy culture, as is its promotion of western-style clothes and decorations. The regional museum adds to this image.

TABLE 1: Population of Incorporated Areas, 1901-1971

	1901	1911	1921	1931	1941	1951	1956	1961	1966	1971
Jasper	382	936	1002	1154	1085	1638	1974	2291	2359	2268
Sunrise[1]						222	244	206	153	144
Embassy			100	103	93	107	115	110	70	55
Eldora			38	112	117	105	166	172	227	205
Victory[2]				58	70	78	67			
Big Bear			232	300	244	245	268	246	203	160
Kelly[3]			210	110						
Altheim				310	427	353	395	479	506	489
Roseville						165	196	215	229	208
TOTAL INCORPORATED AREAS	382	936	1640	2159	2044	2902	3358	3719	3747	3529

[1]Incorporated in 1942
[2]Disorganized in 1952
[3]Disorganized in 1934

Source: Census of Canada: 1961 Vol. I, Part 1-10, Table 6; 1971 Vol. I, Part 1-2, Table 2.

Because there is a major effort expended by town residents on lawns and gardens, Jasper stands as a green oasis in this semi-arid grassland. Along tree-lined side streets there are unpretentious wood and brick houses similar in construction to those found in many small western and midwestern towns. The smaller service centres of Embassy and Eldora in the southern part of the region, and Big Bear, Sunrise, and Altheim in the northern part, contrast with Jasper not only in size and services, but also in appearance. They present to the outside observer a dismal scene of rarely painted small stores and small wood houses, with a few grain elevators towering above.

These small villages did, however, offer important services to the local farmers. The towns represented different stages of growth and development: Altheim, Eldora, and Big Bear were larger than Sunrise or Embassy and, although the abandoned businesses and vacant houses still outnumbered the occupied ones, in the early 1960s they seemed to be in the midst of an economic upswing, which continued for Eldora and Altheim into the 1970s. They included the usual elevators, bulk oil dealers and garages as well as grocery and hardware stores. They were also school centres. Big Bear and Altheim had a branch of an eastern Canadian bank and had built, through volunteer labour, curling and skating rinks. Altheim also had an old hotel, poolroom, and barber shop as well as a café.

Altheim is one of the few population centres which shows a slow continual gain in population, a gain due to several factors. First, its location – midway between Leader and Jasper – serves a very large area. Second, in 1968 a sodium sulphate plant constructed nearby brought in about six or seven families and their children. Third, beginning in 1950 and continuing today, Altheim – unlike most of the population centres in the region – provided residences for a number (in 1970 there were fifteen) of "sidewalk farmers" (both full- and part-time operators) who, upon their takeover, decided to live in town rather than on the enterprise.

Embassy and Sunrise were representative of the many towns throughout the prairies which were planned as rail stops and had a short period of prosperity during the height of the homestead period. By the 1960s Embassy consisted of a café, a general store, and a machine repair shop and gas station. There was also a two-room school which served children up to the eighth grade. In 1972 the café, store, and school were closed. A large number of the abandoned houses had been removed and Embassy appeared to be a road stop with nothing but a gas station. Eldora was now the primary service centre.

Sunrise, larger than Embassy, had two grocery stores, a café, and three gas stations. It also boasted a pool hall. In 1972 Sunrise maintained its bulk oil dealer, service stations, and school, but its grocery stores and café had vanished. Unlike Embassy, the previously abandoned houses had been renovated and were occupied by retired farmers and their wives. In addition, several farmers had moved into the town but continued to farm. These surviving villages serve as an important unifying focus for the farmers located on dispersed farmsteads in the surrounding area.

Jasperites also recognize "districts" (neighbourhoods) within the region, which are usually named for past schools or post office stations. These districts have no stable or precise boundaries, but came into being as meaningful social units based upon the organization of schools which served as a focal point for the organization of social life. In the 1960s most of the original districts were no longer centres of social activity due to the loss of population and the closing of the one- and two-room schools. Most older Jasperites regarded district solidarity with nostalgia, talking for hours about the "old days" when everyone came to the school house for weekly dances. With the improvement in transportation, social life has been developing in a more regional pattern which centres around the remaining small town, Cypress Hills Park in the summer and, of course, Jasper town itself.

CHAPTER II

Resources, Consumption, and Reputation

The Jasper agricultural social system, like all others, is an amalgam of interconnecting social networks of kinship, friendship, mutual aid, and economic exchange. Within the region there are distinctive ethnic-occupational groups: ranchers, farmers, townspeople, Hutterites, and Indians, each of whom has important behavioural markers which serve to maintain their distinctiveness.

Jasper rural society lacks a rigid stratification system and a ranked status system. The Jasper agriculturalist will rarely make a judgment as to social rankings of others or himself. Instead, he makes distinctions in terms of associational patterns such as "He's mixed up with all those ranchers", or in terms of ethnic background such as "All those Scandinavians stick together". District residence, along with religious affiliation, serves to segregate people into social groups or types. Comments such as "She's Catholic, you know", or "We're from the south" (the southern portion of the region), or "Z- is from Embassy . . . they're

---

[1] A portion of this section was presented with John W. Bennett at the Mid-West Sociological Association Meetings, Madison, Wisconsin, May 1966, under the title, "The Social Stratification System of a Post-Frontier Society."

very cliquish", serve as identification. The Jasperite differentiates between country and town, as well as between ranch and farm, or the nature of one's agricultural enterprise. Although they hesitate to rank one another, Jasper agriculturalists will comment upon an individual's lack of, or excess of, resources. There are the "two-bit" places (very small and marginal enterprises) and there are "the big guys" (very large enterprises). There is general agreement – although this was more common in the early 1960s than in the 1970s – that ranching has higher status than does farming. As one woman put it:

> All of our income comes from cattle, but if we say we're a ranch then people think you're putting on the dog.

The higher ranking of ranch over farm is a consequence in part of the romanticization by the media of the cattleman as hero. It is also an aspect of the prestige given to the early settlers who were, for the most part, cattlemen. In large part, however, it is a reflection of the economic realities of the region: the rancher does have more land and is economically more secure than is the farmer.

Table 2 presents the differences in acreage which existed in the two time periods (1962 and 1972) between the three major enterprise types: grain, diversified (mixed grain and livestock), and livestock.

TABLE 2: Mean Acreage: 1962-1972

	1962	1972	Acreage Change	% Change
Grain	1084 (n=27)	1373 (n=20)	+ 289	+27%
Diversified	1886 (n=89)	2410 (n=63)	+ 724	+38%
Livestock	7373 (n=35)	8447 (n=47)	+1074	+14%

Table 3 presents the differences in the "calculated gross income" which existed in the two time periods (1962 and 1972) between the three enterprise types.

TABLE 3: Mean Calculated Gross Income*

	1962	1972	Change	% Change
Grain	11,875 (n=24)	17,177 (n=18)	+ 5302	+45%
Diversified	12,712 (n=73)	20,119 (n=46)	+ 7405	+58%
Livestock	26,603 (n=29)	48,378 (n=33)	+21,775	+81%

*The "calculated gross income" has been derived from the gross income received from the sales of agricultural produce. It was compared with the reported actual income received from agricultural production by half of our sample population. In all cases, the reported income was similar or identical to the calculated income. It does not include other sources of income which may come from occasional sales of dairy products or garden produce or income derived from interest or rent.

The disparity in income and land was particularly glaring in the early period of homestead settlement before political action by farmers to equalize the distribution of resources was successful[2] – political activities which continue into the contemporary period. The provincial government's response has been the development of cooperative utilization of resources, one of which has been the establishment of community pastures and cooperative grazing facilities for cattle. In 1962 diversified cattle producers had access to an average of 1003 acres. In 1972 the mean was 1220 acres, an increase of 22 percent.[3] The development of cooperative mechanisms to control resources by farmers, although successful in the establishment of community grazing pastures and irrigation districts, was still very recent in 1962-1963, and even with cattle production, the financial stability of the farmer was not assured. By 1972, although disparities in income and acreage still persisted, the generalized ranch-farm hierarchy was less an issue of note.

The regional society does talk in general terms about the "bigness" of an agricultural operator, referring broadly to his income, his resources, and the level of development of his enterprise. These are all public markers of an economic position which excludes women. Women are, of course, part of the social ranking system of the region, but since they are not the primary producers, their position in this scheme is derived from, and dependent upon, their relationships to the men who are ranked – the husband or father.

It should be made clear that the total number of acres and a man's gross income are only approximations of the resources available for use by the producer. While they indicate one aspect of relative economic ranking, they bear little relation to how a family lives. What is left over for the household may be very little indeed.

Jasper agriculturalists in the early 1960s lived frugally with few consumption luxuries. While virtually everyone had electricity and an electric freezer, not everyone had running water or an indoor toilet. Of course, some families had "everything", but these were few. In the following table the index of relative consumption is based upon two areas of consumption: household furnishings[4] and personal possessions.[5]

---

[2] See C. Schwartz, *The Search for Stability: Contemporary Saskatchewan* (Toronto: McClelland and Stewart, 1959); S. M. Lipset, *Agrarian Socialism* (Garden City, New Jersey: Anchor Books, 1968); also V. C. Fowke, *The National Policy and the Wheat Economy* (Toronto: University of Toronto Press, 1957).

[3] The number of enterprises on which these percentages are based is as follows: 1962, n = 35; 1972, n = 29.

[4] The ratings given for household furnishings were based upon the presence or absence and the condition of the following items: age of house, running hot water, indoor toilet, furnishings, kitchen and laundry appliances.

[5] The ratings given for personal possessions were based upon the presence or absence of the following items: boat, vacation cabin, stereo, piano (or organ), antiques, movie or 35mm camera, and tape recorder.

TABLE 4: Level of Consumption, 1962-1972

Consumption Level	1962 No.	%	1972 No.	%
Very High	2	1	5	5
High	17	12	21	21
Medium	48	34	36	37
Low	49	35	25	26
Very Low	25	18	11	11
TOTAL	141	100	98	100

Holidays are another form of consumption (see Table 5). The greatest percentage of change between the 1960s and 1970s has been in the increased regularity of holidays which Jasperites take.

TABLE 5: Regularity of Holidays Taken Within Past Five Years

	1962 No.	%	1972 No.	%
Holidays Taken				
Regularly	18	15	30	35
Not Regularly	46	40	34	40
Never	52	45	21	25
TOTAL	116	100	85	100

Looking at the consumption tables we see that the greatest increase in the percentage of change has been in the "high" category, while the greatest decrease in the percentage of change has been in the "low" category. In the early 1960s Jasper agriculturalists were investing virtually all of their discretionary income into the enterprise so that little was left over for any consumption. It is in the late 1960s that there is change — not only in consumption levels, but in the use of credit for consumption items, a procedure heretofore used only for the enterprise. In this we can say Jasper has joined the rest of the consumption society.

Social Esteem or Reputation

Despite change in the consumption patterns in Jasper during the decade, the way in which a man or woman manages consumption wants remains important as one of those qualities which comprise a person's social esteem or reputation within the region. One's reputation is a composite of several behavioural qualities — "character traits" — which are considered important by Jasperites. The degree to which one demonstrates them gives one a reputation, or what we have called social credit. These qualities are similar for men and women, although the actions which validate these qualities differ for the sexes. They are:

Good family man; Good housekeeper and mother. A man who is a good provider; good to his wife and children. A woman who maintains a reasonably clean house; who can feed her family and any others well; whose children are "well behaved".

Good worker. One who is not lazy; who does the job without complaining and who is competent in the necessary skills.

Good manager. An efficient and relatively successful operator of an enterprise or operator of a household. One who knows what to do with money; who does not waste it on "useless" things.

Good neighbour; Good friend. A pleasant, helpful, and sociable person; one who helps when necessary and does it with friendship. One who does not press for reciprocity or gossip about another's failings.

Independent. One who is self-reliant; who takes help only when necessary; who displays initiative and enterprise.

There is a second aspect of the "independence" factor which we have called "hardship prestige". The person to whom this is attributed has "stuck it out" through drought and depression. "Hardship prestige" is one form of credit which most of the wealthy can never have; hence they seek to substitute other symbols of "independence" and "self-reliance".[6]

A man is evaluated by his associates primarily in terms of his relationship to his enterprise, whose type defines to a large degree his associational networks and identifies him to others. Therefore, a man's status or position shifts relative to how he handles his enterprise and the fortunes of that particular enterprise.

Although a man's reputation as an efficient operator is commonly considered to be independent of his wife's reputation as a competent household manager, without her aid in terms of labour and managerial skills he would not be able to develop the kind of relationships with others which are necessary to establish himself as a "good" man. Demonstration of "goodness" as a family man, as a manager, or as a neighbour involves deployment of all available resources within the family enterprise. The role the wife takes within the enterprise, her demands upon the resources of the enterprise, or her support of the husband's expectations concerning the participation of children in the enterprise will have a considerable effect upon the husband's reputation. Of course, the woman has a vested interest in securing the husband's reputation,

---

[6] Those young men who have inherited large productive enterprises are watched carefully to see what they will do. They are considered to have been born "with silver spoons", but this high economic status does not mean they have esteem. They must demonstrate their own worth. If they choose to do little in terms of the enterprise, their status declines; the regional residents scornfully talk about so-and-so "just sitting on all that land".

since it reflects upon herself and also assists in securing the needed resources.

As noted earlier, women, unlike men, have both a *derived* and an *achieved* position within the region. Women derive their economic status position in terms of their relationship to those men with whom they are linked (either as daughter, wife, mother), men who are given public accord for the operation and development of an enterprise. One consequence of this practice is that a woman's family lineage is more important throughout her lifetime in "placing" her within the regional stratification system than is that of a man. Also, the woman's position as an instrumental support for her husband is reinforced where her lineage can contribute important economic and social resources.

At the same time, women have personal reputations which are achieved independently of the men with whom they may be linked. A woman's personal reputation is based upon her demonstration of those behaviours which are defined by the larger region as "good"; these behaviours, for the most part, are acted out in the domestic sphere.[7] However, it should be noted that since the domestic sphere is not isolated from the public or male enterprise sphere, and since the man's reputation is to an important degree dependent upon his wife, Jasper women (and, in fact, all women in family agricultural enterprises) have a uniquely pivotal role in the system which has been ignored for the most part by both rural sociologists and agricultural public policy makers.

Power

Power is defined in terms of "getting what one wants". This use is similar to Adams' definition of power in terms of "the control that is exercised by a party over the environment of another party."[8] The better the reputation a man has as an efficient operator, the better are his chances of getting what he wants from the government bureaus which regulate access to leaseland and irrigation, since the bureaus take into account a man's local reputation in their assignments of land and water. Similarly, the better the reputation a man has in terms of the character traits considered important by the Jasper agriculturalist, the more likely it is that he will be given aid or special consideration, for example, loans or additional labour when he needs it.

---

[7] The fact that women's personal reputations are based upon performance in nonpublic areas is common to most societies. In her discussion of this, Rosaldo notes the cross-cultural comparability of women's roles. She writes: "Men are, in a real sense, identified with and through those groups of kin or peers that cut across domestic units; ranked in hierarchies of achievement, they are differentiated in their roles.-These systems of ranking, grouping, and differentiation comprise the explicit social order that social scientists typically describe. Women, for their part, lead relatively comparable lives, both within a culture and from one culture to the next." Rosaldo, *op. cit.*, p. 29.

[8] Richard N. Adams, *The Second Sowing* (San Francisco: Chandler Publishing Co., 1967), p. 32.

The woman controls important spheres of action which are relevant for the development of the enterprise and also for her husband's reputation as the publicly defined enterprise head. She can exercise control within the family household through her management skills in household efficiency or through what we have called "social relation skills" – competencies which serve to ensure the smooth operation of the group. She can exercise control outside of the family household through her personal connections to other households in the region, through her knowledge of the resources which are available,[9] and through her competence in dealing with external bureaucratic agencies.

The younger man starting out will be judged by the kind of relationships he has with others and his ability – as well as that of his wife – to work hard and delay gratification. These qualities are essential if he hopes to obtain loans and information from the local banker and government agents in charge of agricultural resources. For example, one young man, son of a local farmer who did not have sufficient acreage for two families, demonstrated his ability as a hard worker by working for surrounding ranchers and by doing harvest work on farms. After a four-year period, he was given the opportunity to take over a farm from an old homesteader. This is his account as recorded in our field notes:

> One day I was helping brand at L-'s . . . on a Sunday it was. G- (the retiring farmer) was there, too, helping out. He called me over . . . Father had spoken to him before, I guess . . . and he said, "I hear you want to buy my place." And that's all there was to it. He was awful nice about it. When I took over, he had some wheat standing, and he told me to go ahead and harvest it and use it for a down payment.

The young man saw it as "luck": "I was here in the right place when he was ready to retire, just lucky, I guess." The older man saw it as preventing one of those "big guys" from getting more and as helping out a good friend's son, a fine young man. Furthermore, the factor of family backing assured payment by the young man.

From the standpoint of the qualities which are considered important for high social esteem, this young man rated high on all. He was pleasant and sociable; always willing to help; a good husband with a fine wife who met all of the regional definitions of "good"; neither was lazy; and both were independent and careful with money. A quote from an interview with him in 1964 illustrates these qualities:

> We [Note the use of "we"] never went into debt, always use cash. We built the house ourselves . . . I put all my own labour into every-

---

[9] See Marvin Sussman and B. E. Cogswell, "Interpersonal Competence: An Issue in Cross-national Family Research," in M. B. Sussman and B. E. Cogswell, eds., *Cross-National Family Research* (Leiden: E. J. Brill, 1972), pp. 205-222.

> thing I can ... do all my own machine repairs. ... We stay away from these pleasure things ... try not to buy them and if we do, we pay cash. No point in paying interest on things which do not pay off. It's different with farm machinery ... it pays for itself, because it lets you do a better job of farming. ... We never buy new cars either — just the old ones, and I repair them myself.

Since the system is open and since reputation is not fixed, but is dependent upon what a man or a woman does, the system allows for change. Men and women can alter their reputations by changing their behaviour, and they will be credited with this change. This "credit", in turn, has consequences for other relationships important for the access to resources. Thus there is continuity with the open, nonstratified frontier society. However, it is important to remember that the character of "open" is relative. Although resources have been redistributed to enable some parity, they are, nevertheless, finite and restricted, making wealth the least amenable to change. In this sense, Jasper is a part of the larger Canadian social system.

CHAPTER III

The Making of a Social Community: The Role of Women

The role women have played on the North American frontier, while not ignored, has been stereotyped and neglected.[1] Historians have rarely focused on the daily lives of ordinary people,[2] and this is where women's part in frontier history is to be found.

An account of the settlement process of Jasper could be written in terms of a generalized societal framework without reference to the individuals who were involved, for example, the advent of the railway in 1883 as initiating Jasper's settlement. However, that type of history presents a national perspective and our concern is with the local, the

---

[1] Veronica Strong-Boag, "Cousin Cinderella: A Guide to Historical Literature Pertaining to Canadian Women," in Marylee Stephenson, ed., *Women in Canada* (Toronto: New Press, 1973), pp. 262-290. Strong-Boag has compiled a set of useful resources for the study of women in Canadian settlement and history. She notes that while the heroic figure of the frontier woman has been a by-product of the frontier thesis, the analysis of the female experience in Canadian history (as in other settings) has been minimal.

[2] Sheila Rowbotham, *Hidden From History* (New York: Random House, 1974). Also see Dorothy E. Smith, "Women, the Family and Corporate Capitalism," in Stephenson, ed., *op. cit.*, pp. 5-35.

everyday world of the settling population. These are people confronting problems, making decisions, searching for alternatives. From these acts local "history" is made, social policy is instituted, and the social environment evolves. With this emphasis, the role women have played emerges more clearly, setting a framework for the understanding of the position of the contemporary Jasper woman.

The data on which this chapter is based comes from the oral and recorded accounts of the daily routines of life on the frontier. Many of the written accounts have been culled from the numerous district history books which were compiled by local women's clubs[3] for the Saskatchewan Jubilee and published locally. Most of these accounts emphasize family history: births, deaths, marriages, the establishment of the family enterprise, and the development of those social amenities which are important for community life (for example, a post office, store, school, roads, and mutual aid). They are strongly *local* in detail – it is the private rather than the public facet of life which is described. Only periodically do external events appear in the accounts, as in the coming of the railway, electrification, irrigation, and relief agencies. We are made to see these public events as responses to the needs and demands of this local population, as well as the means whereby links with the national social structure are forged.[4]

We can distinguish two major periods of settlement of the Jasper region: the first, prior to the opening of the region for homesteading, extends from the late 1870s to 1905-1906; the second occurs after 1906 and the closing of the open range for cattle. The latter period, a time of heavy homesteading in all parts of the region, continues until the early 1920s.

Settlement Phase I: Pre-Homestead Cattlemen

The first settlers were cattlemen, for the most part Americans who worked for large ranching companies in the United States and who glimpsed the possibilities of establishing themselves on the empty Canadian Plains. There were also young Englishmen – often "remittance men" – or eastern Canadians who came West with the Mounted Police

---

[3] It is common for women – or one woman in particular – in a family to accept the responsibility of keeping the genealogical information on the family. See Raymond Firth, Jane Forge, and Anthony Hubert, *Families and Their Relations* (London: Humanities Press, 1970). In this case, women have accepted the responsibility of acting as "scribes", the recorders of history – the "culture bearers".

[4] For a theoretical account using Jasper data, see J. W. Bennett, "Microcosm-Macrocosm Relationships in North American Agrarian Society," *American Anthropologist*, 69(1968), 441-454.

or drove supplies for the survey party of the Canadian Pacific Railway.

This early prehomestead frontier population was (like most frontiers) composed primarily of single young men.[5] They settled in isolated areas of the region, near protected coulees along creeks. They were not bound – as was the later farm homesteader – to the geometric grids which ignored natural terrain and physical resources. The rancher, even where there were women and children, had no expectations of urban amenities such as stores, schools, and medical care. They expected to provide for themselves or, if they were not aware of the situation, they soon recognized it. When necessary, they moved into town (Jasper). One pioneer records:

> In the fall of 1891 I was born. Having no nearby neighbour or hospital, arrangements were made for a room at the International Hotel in town (Jasper) with Mrs. H- – a local midwife – and the doctor from the barracks (RCMP).

In that first prehomestead generation, families were isolated for months at a time. However, "families" included aged parents, unmarried siblings and, in some instances of larger ranch outfits, the wives of hired hands who worked with the ranch wife. Nevertheless, women were not uncommonly without the company of another woman in those early days, so that the arrival of a new bride (or sister, or mother) was greeted with joy, as one early pioneer recalled:

> The ranching district was fairly well settled at that time (1894) – all were bachelors (except the man who is recounting the history). When T- brought his wife and family out from England, Mrs. D- was thrilled to have another woman in the area.

The ideological cost could be lessened by establishing the ability to live alone as a "good";[6] the social cost by the rewards of visiting and the demonstrations of hospitality.

Many reminiscences emphasize the active social life. One man recalled:

---

[5] Richard A. Bartlett, *The New Country* (New York: Oxford University Press, 1974), p. 342.

[6] The acceptance of isolated living is consistent with many a contemporary rancher's attitude toward town and urban living which he still describes variously as "cooped in a pen" or "fenced in" or "like being caged". The older ranchers (the settling generation) distinguish between those ranchers who settled near town and those in the "bush". As one grand old lady put it, the rancher near town just wasn't a "real rancher": "I don't think of Jasper (town) area as a real ranch community. That's a different community life there than the one we had. They're all smaller ranchers – no big ones. A lot of the kids went to school in Jasper. They would let the cattle go and not feed in the winter the way we did. They would sit around and talk all winter in Jasper." And indeed, many of the early (pre-1900) ranchers near town called themselves "farmers" (this was before the romanticization of the West) and many businessmen combined cattle raising with storekeeping and horsetrading.

> The pioneers made their own entertainment with concerts, picnics, and dances. The talent for the concerts was provided by anyone who might have the gift of reciting poetry, singing, or step-dancing. A picnic to the pine bush (now the Cypress Park) was a gay occasion with everyone on their favourite saddle horse. Dances were held with dancers staying for breakfast. The babies and younger children were put to sleep on the pile of coats that were on the beds. A babysitter was unknown in those days. It was at such a dance that G-P- was accused of leaving one of his many children amid the covers and did not miss the child until the next day.

The ranch man was less isolated than were the women and children, since he had a work crew of at least one other man. In addition, a man was always welcome to stop along the way at a neighbour's place for a meal or to bed down for the night. Although the physical need for such hospitality has lessened, this visiting pattern persists: the contemporary rancher will "stop in" and eat dinner, and exchange news and shoptalk about cattle with a neighbour on his way to or from another errand. These visits, which serve both social and business functions, are regarded by the ranching population as important indicators of their friendliness and helpfulness to others and place in relief their independence from temporal constraints in contrast to the town businessman.

Since the ranch population was widely dispersed due to extensive land use, ranch families were forced to find individual solutions to problems such as schooling for children. For example, since the establishment of a school required a minimum of ten children, in the frontier period – and even after the influx of homesteaders – the more isolated districts in the Cypress Hills lacked a sufficient number. One early settler wrote:

> For a number of years we tried to get a school started, as our two girls were then old enough to go to school. But as yet there were not enough children in the district to form a school and I had to keep teaching them at home. In about 1919, H-O- moved into the district and his children, with a few others already there, gave us enough....

The solutions to this particular problem varied: in some cases, the mothers and the children moved to Jasper for the winter; in a few cases the children either boarded in town or lived by themselves, with a fifteen-year-old acting as head of the household. Such a decision depended upon the mother's value to the ranching operation and how important schooling was considered for children. In some situations, particularly where there were large families, the rancher hired a teacher who lived with the family. Sometimes neighbouring ranchers with children helped pay so that their children could travel to the ranch house for lessons. If the mother had some formal education, she might act as teacher, usually taking advantage of correspondence courses. One pioneer recalls:

> School was a problem, for my folks lived seven miles from the nearest school. We took correspondence courses up to grade eight, hiring a girl to teach us. This proved a chore keeping a teacher as it wouldn't be long before they would get married.... Later to get to school we rode, boarded out, lived in a little log shack and stayed in town....

The increased number of settlers after the full opening of the region for homesteading in 1910 made possible community solutions to the problem. The early rancher, remembering his personal solutions, was in some cases hostile and resentful of the new emigrants making demands for social amenities which he and his family had done without. However, he ignored the fact that the Royal Canadian Mounted Police provided him and his family with many social services — from mail-carrying to doctors — and the fact that he was beneficiary of an enormous public resource: miles of land on which he grazed his private cattle.[7]

Settlement Phase II: Homestead Farm

The homestead farming population also had many young, single men, but differed from the ranch population in that it had a larger component of women and children.

The greater numbers of women and children created demands for social amenities based upon their past experiences of nucleated settlement. They wanted schools, churches, stores, and the establishment of a community social life. The demand for schools and their establishment created a focal point for the homestead farm community. One pioneer recalled:

> In 1916, the West Plains School was built. I was appointed secretary for the board and was a member of the board for nine years. The school became the centre of our social life; for church services, concerts, box socials, wedding receptions and even a wedding....

Farmers never valued isolation. Houses were built with access to neighbours and to the road. Where the rancher resented the intrusion of the homesteader upon "his" range,[8] the homesteader watched with eager interest the incoming neighbours. A pioneer noted:

> When we first come out, there was not a house to be seen on the whole prairie for as far as the eye could reach, but now we could

---

[7] Nellie Rabourne, "Why There is a Feud Between Ranchers and Farmers," *The Western Producer,* May 28, 1964.
[8] Prior to the closing of the range for homesteading, the rancher had no competition for grazing resources, since his cattle were free to roam at will.

see shacks going up all over, yes, and little by little we got to know quite a few people....

The homestead farm population came to build a society. They were on a frontier, but the frontier experience was considered only a phase in a development process. One woman wrote:

> ... all were pioneering and knew what it meant: undying, undaunted hope for the future of the country. There was a real desire and determination to see the country progress and to stay with it, to see the railroad come in, see towns spring, and of course many years later, the farm electrification and the many usual evidences of progress.

The importance of the development of the small towns is reiterated as early settlers recall their homestead experiences:

> In the summer of 1914 the school children were given a half-holiday ... the day the C.P.R. laid down the steel through the Village of Embassy. We had two miles to go, but with joy we ran along and had plenty of time to see the steel laid down on the new dirt grade. Before this Mrs. S- had built a new shop on the town site and Mr. H- a store. Mrs. F- had started a restaurant. People were building everywhere — stores, more restaurants, laundry, hotel, bank. Every week a couple of new places opened for business. Embassy was really progressing with its new hospital, school. ... People everywhere and prosperity for all.

Of course, the establishment of a town and its amenities required sufficient population, and the heavy settlement of the prairie districts in the region made towns possible — albeit not for very long. This heavy settlement became a kind of ecological catastrophe, and only a few years after the establishment of the small towns, crop failures led to the abandonment of homesteads and the failure of town businesses:

> Embassy had about everything. Like most towns in a new country it attracted every kind of business. Some hopeful men ... built a hall but after a few years found it to be a losing proposition and let it go to the village for taxes....

The responses to the situation took both public and private forms. Demands required governmental agencies to furnish relief and new resources: irrigation programs, grazing programs, and collective marketing were all part of the governmental response. On the other hand, large-scale migration[9] from the region was the common personal solution. But for those who stayed, the daily routines of life were in a sense simply a prolongation of the frontier period. Women were faced with

---

[9] S. W. Alty, "The Influence of Climate and Other Geographic Factors on the Growth and Distribution of Population in Saskatchewan," *Geography,* 24 (1939), 10-33.

the problems of having enough water and of feeding, clothing, and schooling their family; men had to maintain an enterprise in the face of severe deprivation.

The Frontier Experience

The experience of the frontier and the drought and depression period called forth extraordinary resources from both men and women. Nevertheless, in the recollections of the past there is a sense of nostalgia. A woman wrote of the nineteen-thirties in the language of the frontier period:

> In one way such hard times were good for a community, as folks made their own fun. Visited around in their Bennett Buggies[10] and shared. Card parties, social evenings and dances were the usual thing. There were no shows, no driving fifty miles to some show or dance. Those were the days when away we would go with lots of robes, blankets and hot rocks in cutters or bob-sleighs; where there was no such thing as babysitters; where young and old danced to Darling Nellie Grey and Red Wing and Clementine....

In a different account a man wrote:

> Those early settlers with their large families had a very hard struggle, and many untold heart-breaking experiences came to everybody's door. Many tears were shed during pioneer days. There was one good thing — we were all in the same boat. When it came to distress and sorrow, friendship and the neighbourly spirit was a wonderful thing in those early years. We had many pleasant evenings at some homes or had dances or card games in the school house. It all helped to make me forget the daily task.

The nostalgia in such accounts is for "community", for the social occasions which provided virtually the only respite from toil. Neighbours, however, provided more than social occasions; they were crucial for survival. One man related:

> Early one morning in midsummer (1910) we were awakened by a knock on the door, and opening it we found a little girl, daughter of Mr. R-, a rancher east of us. She had been sent to ask help of us to fight a fire that had been started from a careless smoker south of us. We took the team and water barrels and started for the fire. Most all the men in the country were there helping.

Many discussions of frontier settlement have emphasized pioneer characteristics of individualism and self-reliance. However, it is impor-

---

[10] This was a car with the engine removed (no money for gas) and hitched to a horse.

tant to remember that cooperation and mutual aid were as common and certainly as important for survival.¹¹ One man recalled:

> In 1917 we moved our shack from the northwest corner of the homestead up on the hill to the east, to higher ground. I worked with O-R- quite a bit; he was a grand neighbour. Before I got my own horses, I could borrow a team from him any time to haul wood, etc. In those days, neighbours depended a great deal on each other.

Neighbourly cooperation was not only important for the establishment of an agricultural enterprise, but provided the resources for personal and household survival needs. One woman, a new bride of three months who had recently arrived in the district, recalled:

> My first experience (1912) was unexpected. The S- were our nearest neighbours. In the small hours of the morning of October 14th, B- came knocking on the door, asking if I would go help his wife, who was in childbirth. I had no experience along these lines, but I went with him. It was a dark, windy night, with only the light from his shack to guide us across the pasture, and we were on foot. Everything went fine, and after an early breakfast, I told B- to take our team and buggy and go into Eldora for the doctor. (B- had only oxen.) The doctor said I had done well. . . .
>
> In February 1924, Mrs. B- came down from the hills to be near the doctor when her baby was born. However, on March 28 the stork arrived before we had time to go for the doctor, so I performed the duties of midwife a second time. . . . I assisted at two more births some years later.

Of course not all survived, and virtually every family had its personal tragedy, due either to lack of medical care or accident[12]

---

[11] John W. Bennett and Seena Kohl, "Characterological, Strategic and Institutional Interpretations of Prairie Settlement," in A. W. Rasporich ed., *Western Canada: Past and Present* (Calgary: McClelland and Stewart West Limited, 1975), pp. 14-27.

[12] We have no infant mortality rates earlier than 1921 for Saskatchewan. However, the mean rate for 1921-1925 is 83.2 (infant deaths under one year of age per 1000 live births) with a range between 76 and 92. Infant mortality rates decline slowly as follows:

Years	Mean Infant Mortality Rate
1926-1930	73.2
1931-1935	61.8
1936-1940	55.0
1941-1945	46.4
1946-1950	40.4
1951-1955	31.6
1956-1960	26.2
1961-1965	26.0
1966-1970	24.2
1971-	20.0

Women on the Frontier

Richard Bartlett, in one of the few historical accounts which mentions the roles women played on the frontier, takes issue with the commonly held view of the frontier woman as overworked and overburdened, a figure of pity. He writes:

> For many of them the transition from life in a settled area to life in a new country was not traumatic. From the status of farmer's daughter to that of pioneer's wife was no great hurdle. The pioneer woman knew that a clearing would have to be made, a cabin built and a community of neighbours created. But these tasks she understood.[13]

Even where they had not the rural background, it is useful to remember that the woman's world of the 1900s was primarily a lifetime of work centred around household duties. Bartlett writes:

> ... the vast majority were wives and mothers. They had in common a way of life covered in one word: toil. They cooked and baked, sewed and knitted, milked cows, tended gardens and raised children. All of this they were expected to do.[14]

He suggests that the frontier offered women new opportunities just as it did for men, that in contrast with the view of the frontier woman as a woman to be pitied, "the new country woman held her head high, and her bright eyes searched the horizon for what lay ahead. She shared with her husband a faith in their future, in the 'great day acomin'' which they would live to see. Beneath her linsey-woolsey or calico frock was a sturdy body. She could walk to Kentucky, or Missouri, or the Pike's Peak country, or to Zion at Salt Lake or to Oregon. She was a builder, along with her husband; she knew her value. If her life was hard, and it was, so was that of her husband. Yet both found life rewarding."[15]

The frontier, despite the hardship involved, certainly provided the opportunity to contemplate a chance for a better life, if not for themselves, then for their children. For women, as for men, the opportunity to own land represented the opportunity of a lifetime. One Jasper pioneer woman recalls:

> Move to Canada the land of "opportunity", so read the headlines in the Kansas papers in 1909. Land was so high-priced in Kansas that one could not afford to buy it so we came to Canada to homestead. "We" being my husband, myself, also my mother and father, two brothers, and a friend....

---

[13] Bartlett, *op. cit.*, p. 351.
[14] *Ibid.*, p. 354.
[15] *Ibid.*, p. 350.

And another:

> My mother, who at that time was Mrs. L-B-, had been left a widow during the winter of 1908. The following spring and summer great news spread far and near, announcing that vast areas of land had been thrown open for homesteading in Saskatchewan. Friends and relatives were greatly excited and enthused over the prospect of obtaining a half section of land for practically *nothing*. This resulted in mother, along with her three brothers ... and three brothers-in-law, as well as friends from different parts of North Dakota, going to Moose Jaw in July to file on homesteads.

The image of a woman which emerges from these accounts highlights the exigencies of the frontier and the fact that, as in other crisis situations, there is a loosening of sex-role expectations.[16] The requirements for survival necessitated the learning of new skills and the putting aside, or holding in abeyance, the traditional concepts of feminine behaviour. Thus one woman who spent a winter on the homestead while her husband worked as a carpenter in Regina recalled:

> The winter I stayed on our homestead alone I shall never forget. Good thing I was young, with lots of courage and ambition and afraid of nothing. I must admit it would have been most lonely many times if it had not been for Mrs. P-, our neighbour a half mile north. The rest of our neighbours were bachelor boys ... they were very kind to me that winter. When we were invited to Mrs. P-'s for dinners or parties either R- or A- would call for me and carry Helen, the baby. We had some real good times together....

Obviously, ideas about intimate social and sexual relationships between young married women and the neighbouring bachelor boys had to be held in abeyance.[17]

Similarly held in abeyance were other concepts of what was "proper" for women:

> Mrs. M-, like many women of that day, was a woman of resourcefulness. She could take a hammer and nails, make a screen door, a go-cart for a baby, pen for the pigs or anything... I remember that summer the grasshoppers were quite bad ... Mr. M- and brother F- would take shovels and throw the bait from the democrat while Mrs. M- drove the team up and down the field....

Another account related:

> There being only one boy – B- – in the family, M- and her sister

[16] Jean Lipman-Blumen, "Role De-differentiation as a System Response to Crisis: Occupational and Political Roles of Women," *Sociological Inquiry*, 43(1973), 105-129.

[17] This is a theme explored by novelist Sinclair Ross, "The Painted Door," in A. Lucas, ed., *Great Canadian Short Stories* (New York: Dell Publishing Co., 1971), pp. 96-115. It is an area in which the potential complications have never been openly discussed.

... had to dust off their own broncs and help with the outside work. In those days the wolves helped to entertain them but they returned the compliments by trapping and shooting themselves a few. ...

The loosening of sex-role definitions did not release women from their primary tasks: the maintenance of the household and the care of children. However, it did permit greater variation from accepted behaviour and ideology – a tendency which continues to this day. Perhaps most important, it permitted women release from the restricted and meaningless role in which they had been placed during the nineteenth century.[18]

The frontier period set the standards for the ideal female role: a woman should be resourceful and "do what has to be done". But at the same time, women are expected to "make a home", a concept which implies warmth and comfort and the niceties of life, a phrase which includes literacy skills and "cultural" attributes such as music, books, and church attendance.[19] Accounts of early women pioneers link homecraft, literacy, and music:

> She was a wonderful cook and home manager. She fed everyone who landed around meal time. On Sundays all the family headed for church where she played the organ and led the singing.

> If little Mrs. M- thought she had worked hard in her childhood, she soon learned that marriage was no escape. She now had the responsibility of a home and an ambitious husband anxious to make good. Her duties seemed to increase. Hungry hired men required good filling meals. The frequent trips to deliver meat (he supplied meat to the RCMP barracks) took her husband away from home several days each week. But she proved equal to her tasks and in after years related many an interesting event. She loved music and dancing and often supplied the former for the country dances via violin and piano, by ear.

There is a duality in the expectations for women which is elaborated by the homestead frontier experience: the emphasis is upon women being resourceful and able to work "like a man", while at the same time remaining "women", responsible for creating a home and a cultural atmosphere.[20]

[18] Audrey Y. Morris suggests this in her account of the Strickland family in *Gentle Pioneers* (Toronto and London: Hodder and Stoughton Ltd., 1971.)

[19] Bartlett writes, "A surprising number of new country women were literate, and it was they who saw to it that the children attended school and Sunday School and did their lessons; in the absence of schools, mother served as teacher. More than that, the women were the ones who reminded the men of the world of literature and the arts." *Op. cit.*, p. 356.

[20] This duality is analagous to other dualities noted in the discussion of the concept of woman. See Sherry B. Ortner, "Is Female to Male as Nature is to Culture?" in Rosaldo and Lamphere, *op. cit.*, pp 67-87.

This dual set of tasks combines both responsibilities in the public spheres – productive work – and responsibilities in the private sphere – maintaining the house and those connected to the household. This combination of tasks is consistent with the dominant pattern of expectations for women throughout history.[21] However, her primary responsibility remains within the household – the private sphere – and she is "freed" from making the process of earning a living her primary concern.[22]

Paradoxically, where women are "freed" from the need to participate in social production, they not uncommonly become important so-

---

The duality in women's roles is symbolized in the ways in which the first generation of women view themselves in relation to town and town events. These women, raised on the frontier, avowed that they hated town and did not go unless they "had" to do so, for town and town women represented boredom, stultification, and pettiness. When they did, they went as befits a "lady", or their conception of a "lady". The following account comes from field notes taken in 1963 before the town of Jasper had paved streets:

"Town was very hot and the wind was blowing dust all over the place in spite of last night's rain which had left some pot holes full of mud – both mud and dust at the same time. I met Mrs. D-, she was dressed to the teeth, a far cry from her usual old pants. There she was in white hat, white shoes, white gloves and stockings – girdled up tightly. She was poised on the sidewalk debating how to cross the street with a minimum of damage to her shoes."

Mrs. D- in town was dressed as townsfolk because, as she said, "When I go to town I'm not going to have anyone talking about me and people thinking just because we live in the bush we're Indians."

On the ranch, Mrs. D- rode, fenced, branded and "did what had to be done" – but she also always served tea in cups and saucers – never mugs – , had lace doilies on her chairs, insisted on a piano so her girls could learn to play, and wore white gloves and stockings to town. (For a general statement of Indian-White relationships, see Niels W. Braroe, *Indian & White* (Stanford: Stanford University Press, 1975).)

[21] Although much of the discussion of woman's roles has placed her only within the home with few exceptions and much rhetoric, she never was *only* there. See Rowbotham, *op. cit.* Also Alice S. Rossi, "Equality Between the Sexes: An Immodest Proposal," *Daedalus* 93,2 (Spring 1964), 607-652.

[22] Of course this "freedom" is only present in those classes where income is sufficient to permit "leisure" from the concern for production. Where women have such options, they are unconnected to the sphere where social rewards are given – they have no control over economic resources and the associated power that comes with this control. See Margrit Eichler, "Women as Personal Dependents," in Stephenson, *op. cit.,* pp. 36-55. It is interesting to note, however, that although they may not have much power within the household, they may wield considerable power outside of the household via the role of the volunteer. This role, associated with the middle-class woman, has been most often viewed as "trivial", in that it is nonproductive, or as another example of exploitation of women. While in many instances these views are essentially correct, they leave out another factor which is involved in women's organizations – the very real issue of power which these groups control in the public arenas as political lobby groups. Furthermore, these organizations also serve as training grounds for political participation of women on a wider scale. See Peter Rossi, "The Organizational Structure of an American Community," in Amitai Etzioni, ed., *Complex Organization: A Social Reader* (New York: Holt, Rinehart and Winston, 1961), pp. 301-312. Also see Margaret E. MacLellan, "History of Women's Rights in Canada," in *Cultural Tradition and Political History of Women in Canada,* Studies of the Royal Commission on the Status of Women in Canada, Report #8 (Ottawa: Information Canada, 1971), pp. 21-24.

cial agents for both cultural development and social change.[23] Children provide much of the rationale for demanding social amenities. In an isolated situation such as a frontier, this function of women becomes even more important.

It is the woman, outside production, who can be concerned with the nonutilitarian social amenities: art, music, dance, literature, and so on. As long as these interests are voluntary (not professional), they are defined as "feminine" attributes. Women accept and elaborate these areas of interest and performance as part of their definitions of self and appraisal of one another. For the frontier woman, this duality has meant that she was not only crucial for the establishment of an agricultural enterprise, but that she had a vital part to play in the social development of a community, and in insisting upon its connection to the larger world.

[23] The role of women as social change agents has been noted elsewhere. See Yolanda and Robert F. Murphy, *Women of the Forest* (New York and London: Columbia University Press, 1974).

CHAPTER IV

Communication Networks & Social Control

Jasper agriculturalists, although they are a dispersed population, desire and need regular social contacts. The problems caused by such dispersed settlement have been lessened by the fact that communication and transportation technology has "shortened" distance, and for many residents this has been one of the more important alterations in daily life. However, along with technological change there have been many social adjustments to sparse population. Jasper agriculturalists have developed social ties that create a closed social space. The low population density has required that individuals interact with one another in a large number of different spheres of action. This creates complex, overlapping relationships.

The term "social redundancy" has been used to describe this phenomenon where "person A is linked to person B not only directly, but also through a number of other individuals."[1] Thus one knows the same person as kinsman, neighbour, brand inspector, municipal councillor.

---

[1] Ronald Frankenberg, *Communities in Britain* (Harmondsworth, Middx.: Penguin Books, Ltd., 1966).

One consequence is that everyone knows everyone else — or at least *about* everyone. Or, given a few social clues, a connection can be established with a known person which then makes the subject relevant. For example, "You know Jan . . . J-L-'s girl, she married the S- boy from Eldora. He worked for J-B- for a short time. His mother was a J-." With these multiple connections there are few impersonal relationships, and the behaviour of everyone is considered relevant and important — at least as a topic of conversation. An effective communication system operates through a series of overlapping networks[2] based upon kinship, friendship, proximity, work associations, and formal organizations. We shall look at each in turn.

Kinship Connections

There were few agricultural households in Jasper not related to others in the region through marriage or descent. The most numerous marriage connections were found between families who were early settlers when marriage was a frequent result of propinquity, a consequence of the limited alternatives and the problems of communication and transportation during that period. We found clusters of intermarrying kin groups (several members of one household marrying members of another) in the more isolated districts of the region (Greenfields and Happydale). Less integrated clusters of intermarrying kin groups were found in the Victory-Eldora-Embassy districts in the southern part of the region, as well as in the heavily homesteaded districts of Sunrise, Big Bear, and Altheim.

With the decreasing isolation of the local districts, brides came from a wider geographic area, although during the research period more than two-thirds of the marriages were still between regional residents (see Table 6).

TABLE 6: Place of Origin of Wives of Agricultural Operators, 1962-1972

Place of Origin	1962 (n=135)		1972 (n=138)	
	No.	%	No.	%
Within Jasper Region				
Born on Farm	82	61	75	54
Born on Ranch	15	11	19	14
Born in Town	6	4	8	6
TOTAL FROM REGION	103	76	102	74
Outside of Jasper				
Region	32	24	36	26

[2] The use of the term "network" follows from Barnes who uses it to trace the social and economic ties among friends, neighbours, and kinsmen. J. A. Barnes, "Class and Committees in a Norwegian Island Parish," *Human Relations*, 7(1954), 39-58.

Marriage serves the important function of linking family groups together into a new relationship. It can, where the circumstances are right, create an entirely new network of kin. The degree to which affinal ties are developed is commonly viewed as open to individual decision. Western society has few rules and regulations governing recognition of affinals beyond the general expectation that there will be continued maintenance of ties with the married couple's families of origin. It is expected that the parents of the newly married couple will incorporate the new nuclear unit into their social sphere, but it is not required that other family members do so. Affinals may recognize one another as related or as kin or in-laws, but such recognition does not mean that they must change their patterns of social interaction to include the new in-laws. Explicitly, this means that the parents of the groom will be criticized for not including the bride with their son in the invitation to Sunday dinner; however, they will not be criticized for not inviting her parents or her sisters and their husbands. Where affinals are incorporated into active social interaction with one another, we can speak of the extension of family ties. David Schneider has used the term "dead end" to describe those relationships which do not include other members of the same family, where there is little social interaction with affinals.

The resources and type of agricultural enterprise are important factors in the extension or nonextension of affinal ties. Thus, although approximately one quarter of the marriages of ranch sons were to farm girls from within the region, the links to the farm population had not been extended to members outside of the girl's nuclear family. In contrast with the ranch son-farm daughter marriages, ranch son-ranch daughter marriages *did* act as interconnecting links which extended beyond the immediate nuclear families involved. In part, this was due to the fact that there already existed more than one marriage link between the ranching families. The newly married served to solidify family ties further. In part, the extension of affinal ties is natural since new in-laws include ranch families with whom other ties, such as labour or machinery exchange, already existed. Similarly, among the farm son-farm daughter marriages, where previous ties of descent and marriage existed, the new marriage served to reinforce these connections. Where there was commonality of interests, consanguinial ties of kinship – which before had been ignored or regarded as "distant" – were reinforced. Thus ties were reinforced between *Ego* (a diversified farmer who is interested in expanding his cattle production), his father-in-law *A* (who is also his father's cousin and a cattle-grain farmer), and his wife's mother's brother *C,* who operates a feed lot (see diagram below).

Ego (and his family) is more involved with these family members than he is with his own sibling who lives outside the region, or his father's brother, a grain farmer in the region who has no interest in cattle.

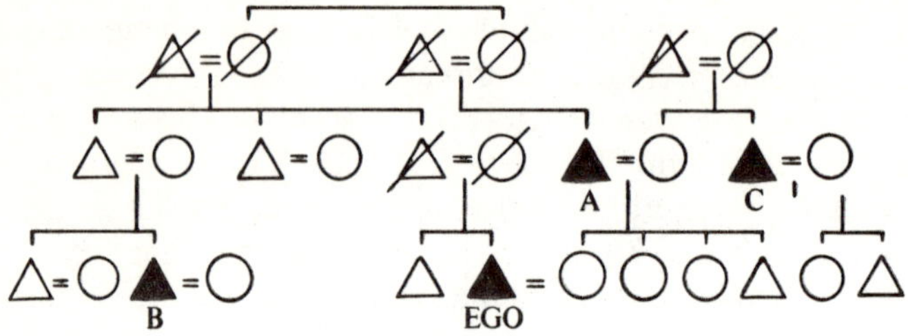

DIAGRAM I: EXTENSION OF KIN TIES

However, there are close social and work ties between *Ego* and his father's brother's son *B*. They are of similar age, their wives are good friends and *Ego*, who is in a favourable situation in terms of land resources, rents land to his cousin *B*. *B* has become more interested in cattle and he, *Ego* and *Ego's* father-in-law *A*, who is also interested in expanding into cattle, form a work-exchange ring. *Ego's* active social participation with *C* is based primarily upon commonality of interests. Their shared economic interests have pulled his wife's family – his affinals – into new social ties.

Formal Organizations

Despite the large number of kinship connections, Jasper social activity is not based primarily upon kinship ties. Even in cases where an organization may consist of members who can all trace kin ties, the organization is not viewed as a kin group. The definition of membership for these groups is based upon common interest and friendship, and the kinship connections of the members are considered as incidental. Participation in voluntary associations is to a large degree based upon sex and locality.

With the exception of the political associations, there are few formal organizations which are not segregated by sex. The men participate in Canadian Legion affairs; the women in the Auxiliary. Men join community service organizations such as the Rotary Club or Kinsmen; the women participate in parallel organizations such as the Kinnettes. Since early settlement, the farm women have established and maintained a series of voluntary organizations which are district-wide rather than regional: Homemaker Clubs, Church Mission groups, and Ladies Aid Societies fall into this category. The Homemaker Club serves to incorporate the diverse religious denominations and its membership thus overlaps that of church-related groups. The young farm or ranch wife participates mainly in the Homemaker Club; therefore, it is not completely dominated by the older women as are the Church and Mission societies. There is also overlapping membership in the church groups, and it is not considered unusual for a woman to belong to both the Mission Group and to the Lutheran Ladies Aid. Catholic farm women have their own organizations, closely affiliated with the Church. These groups not only provide for the women's social needs, but also serve to define and differentiate the particular district as a social unit.

Participation in voluntary organizations provides important sources of social support and recreation for women, the majority of whom are involved in at least one voluntary organization. It is among the ranch women that we find the lowest level of activity (see Table 7), for only in recent years, with the improvement in transportation, was the ranch woman who desired to do so able to attend the usual monthly meetings. However, it is not only an issue of transportation which limits the ranch woman's participation in the traditional women's clubs. For a number of these women, recreational needs are served by their activity in the ranch itself and the ancillary instrumental activities in which they join with others, albeit less formally than in the women's organizations.

Both ranch and farm women, through their participation in associations which are connected to national groups of women, extend their ties outside of the region. By her involvement in national voluntary associations, as well as her maintenance of ties to kinsmen and friends, the geographically isolated resident is incorporated into the national social system and this makes for a middle-class orientation similar to her urban and suburban counterparts. Similarly, the man's participation in political and economic organizations in the search for power and control over resources serves to link him to the national system and to prevent isolation from the urban mainstream of ideas and change.

TABLE 7: Level of Women's Participation in Organizations, 1960-1970

	Very High		Standard		Low		Very Low		Total	
	No.	%	No.	%	No.	%	No.	%	No.	%
1960 Mode of Production										
Grain Farm	–		9	47	7	37	3	16	19	15
Mixed Farm	7	9	40	53	12	16	16	21	75	58
Livestock	–		16	46	8	23	11	31	35	27
	7	5	65	50	27	21	30	23	129	
1970 Mode of Production										
Grain Farm	–		9	64	3	21	2	14	14	12
Mixed Farm	4	8	29	56	12	23	7	135	52	46
Livestock	2	4	17	36	11	23	17	36	47	42
	6	5	55	49	26	23	26	23	113	

Ties of Friendship

The young rancher or farmer is an active participant in a strong network of local ties based on common interest and long-term association. He has grown up with a group of young men who continue to share his work and interests and the old boyhood relationships are easily maintained. The work habits of the rancher lead to greater participation in an all-male social group, since his peers can supply his need for additional labour. The operator without cattle does not have these labour needs, and the farm operator who does have cattle is served by cooperative or community pasture organizations.

The close peer ties of the young men are crosscut by participation in community activities such as curling in the winter and ball games during the summer, community activities which involve children, or the dine and dances held periodically by various fraternal or political organizations, thereby creating a social life which is more heterogeneous for all. Although the operators' social ties of friendship continue throughout their lifespans, as the men age, marry, have children, and assume greater responsibilities for the enterprise, they do not participate as frequently in the all-male age set. The network of friendship for the older rancher will depend greatly upon the ties of friendship which exist between his wife and the wives of his peers. If his wife is associated with the town organizations, it is likely that the rancher's ties will expand to include farm operators and townsmen to a greater degree than before.[3]

The young woman's situation is different, since her primary responsibilities are within the family household. In order to maintain social ties she must make special arrangements which do not coincide with her daily tasks. Thus her participation in organized social groups becomes the most common means whereby she maintains and develops her friendship ties.

Wives of men who are connected by work exchanges and social experiences will often accompany their husbands and use the time to visit. Where wives are not friendly, or where the young man does not live up to the expectations of his father in terms of time spent on the family enterprise, then the active association of men can create friction within the family household.

Economic Exchange

Participation in work exchanges crosscuts kinship and friendship ties and, although much work exchange was based upon friendship ties,

---

[3] This pattern is different from that found among the choice patterns for friends among professionals and business executives, where friendship is associated with the husband's choice. See N. Babchuk and A. P. Bates, "The Primary Relations of Middle Class Couples: A Study of Male Dominance," *American Sociological Review,* 28(1963),377-384.

there were also other cooperative mechanisms as, for example, the grazing cooperatives responsible for haying and branding activities. Less formal work groups, dependent upon proximity and perceived self-interest, emerge between neighbours. These dyadic relationships are termed "neighbouring", and serve an important function in a region where the cash for labour is in short supply.[4] Further, such exchanges become opportunities for social occasions and serve to relieve the monotony of the agricultural operations.

Ranching, with its branding and extensive haying operations, retained more of the traditional group or district exchanges that were common before machinery. The farmers combined socializing with work in the form of machinery demonstrations, but they participated to a lesser degree than the ranchers in this traditional type of work exchange. This is an often noticed difference between farm and ranch operators: the former is tied to his machine, whereas the cattleman has the opportunity for social participation in his economic activity.

Dyadic work exchanges are for the most part relationships between men. Women exchange work independently of the enterprise labour exchanges in areas such as cooking, child care, or care of the sick. When women become involved in the dyadic exchanges of labour for enterprise needs, it is also in these areas. Thus, for example, women will make pies for a branding. During those periods of heavy activity a woman sends her daughter to "help out" if she does not go herself. Of course, she expects reciprocity in those same areas when she has need for it.

Where the women of the neighbouring enterprises are friends or kin, the dyadic work exchanges become important social and recreational outlets in addition to being economically important; however, where the women of the exchanging households are not friends, the enterprise labour exchange serves purely economic functions. The fact that such interaction is not the sum total of the social activities of the participants prevents formation of the tightly knit locality groups that anthropologists associate with peasant populations. In particular, the multiple connections which cut across spheres of activity serve as an important means for the transmission of information and for the maintenance of social ties in a sparsely populated region.

Processes of Communication

In Jasper there is no anonymity and little privacy; talk and speculation about others is constant. Interest in the activities of others can be considered oppressive and a disadvantage of rural or small town life;

---

[4] J. W. Bennett, "Reciprocal Economic Exchanges among North American Agricultural Operators," *Southwestern Journal of Anthropology,* 24(1968),276-309.

but at the same time, contrasted with the impersonalization of the city, it is an indication that people "care" about one another. This is what people mean when they say that Jasper is "safe" and a "good" place to raise children.[5]

The concern for others manifested in part by discussion about others is an extension of the interest and concern one has with one's own family members. Many of the topics for discussion are trivial and of little consequence to those who are not similarly involved. They include such things as a baby's first tooth, toilet training, a new chair cover or haircut. They also involve issues of the domestic group, such as marital or financial problems. As Gluckman[6] has effectively written, gossip about others serves as an important means in the creation and maintenance of social ties. This becomes particularly true where face-to-face interaction may not be easy and thus news about others through conversation takes on this added dimension of maintaining social ties. Consequently, although the Jasper agriculturalist lives on widely dispersed farmsteads where the isolation of houses gives the appearance of considerable privacy, the multiple social ties and the expectations that accompany them establish a very effective communication system.

Because the agricultural enterprise is on continuous public display, the position of the agriculturalist is a particularly open one in contrast with the "closed" nature of other types of business enterprises. The general condition of a man's enterprise and his methods of operation can be determined with considerable accuracy simply by observing from the road the condition of pasturage, cattle, crops, or the particular stage of agricultural activity that an operator is engaged in (for example, haying or fallowing). Such information is carried to town in "casual" conversation. The following passage from field notes illustrates a common occurrence:

> *A* has stopped in at the garage during haying time to get a part for his machine. He mentions to *B*, the garage mechanic, that *C*'s (his neighbour) hay was spread all over the field by the wind last night. *D* stops in at the garage and *B* says, "Say, *A* told me that the wind really made a mess out of *C*'s hay last night." *D* greets *C* outside the garage and says, "I hear you've got a mess on your hayflat . . . that the wind really blew it all over."

---

[5] Jasperites often talked about the shortcomings of the region: the weather; the lack of urban amenities, recreational facilities for young people, and occupational alternatives. Some were disgruntled about the lack of "community spirit" or concern for education or economic development but, with few exceptions, they did not want to move, and virtually all agreed that the values of country life compared favourably with those of town or urban living. They viewed cities (or towns) outside the region as full of too many people who "don't care" in contrast with the friendliness and hospitality of the people of the prairies. This attitude was summed up by one individual as follows:

"I lived in Trail, B.C. during the forties, and I was sure glad to get back here. You can always recognize prairie folks . . . no locked doors . . . no looking down their noses at you and always a friendly hand."

[6] Max Gluckman, "Gossip and Scandal," *Current Anthropology,* 3 (1963), 307-316.

In this sparsely populated region, any car or truck owned by a resident is easily recognized; "foreign" or nondistrict cars are quickly spotted and assigned ownership; and the region's residents know who is visiting whom or who was driving into or away from town. This knowledge is often verified later, for example, "Wasn't *A* over at your place on Tuesday?" Similarly, neighbours know in what field a man will be working, if neighbour *C* needs help, or if friend *A* has helped friend *B* with a particular task.

Men, who are out of the house and away from the farm or ranch more than women, carry news of the countryside when they stop to have coffee with neighbours or when they meet mutual friends in town. Since the women are more restricted to household tasks, they use the telephone for the maintenance of ties. The phone ring itself is a way of gaining knowledge about, or of maintaining contact with, others. Since each house on a party line has a distinct ring, one knows by the ring who is being called and who has or has not answered. (It is assumed that if one does not answer, one is not home.) If a neighbour has information on the whereabouts of the person being called, he will answer the phone and talk with the caller. And because each party expects the others to listen in on party-line calls, what is said is controlled.

The *Jasper News* (published weekly in Jasper town), along with the telephone and car, effectively manages to reduce spatial distances and isolation.[7] The paper provides information about crops, farm commodities on sale in town, and the weather conditions in various parts of the region. It serves as a bulletin board for the community by announcing coming events; as a mailing list for invitations to social functions; and as a means for thanking people for their gifts and services. One can buy an advertisement in order to thank people publicly. For example:

> I wish to thank Dr. S-, nurses and staff of the Jasper Union hospital for the good care and kindness while I was a patient. Thanks also to all the relatives and friends who sent cards, treats and visited me.

The newspaper serves as a major source of information about what residents are doing, since each district in the region has its own correspondent whose reports are published regularly. These faithful reporters tell readers who is visiting whom and who has made trips out of the region, as well as the purpose of the trips. For example:

> Mr. A-M- and his mother, Mrs. J-M-, accompanied by Mrs. E-B-, motored to Saskatoon on Sunday where the latter will be seeking medical attention at St. Paul's Hospital.

---

[7] Miner has written that "the rural paper functions as sort of a formalized 'back-fence chat,' an institutionalization necessitated by the expanded community." See Horace Miner, *Culture and Agriculture: An Anthropological Study of a Corn Belt Country* (Ann Arbor, Michigan: Occasional Contributions from the Museum of Anthropology of the University of Michigan, No. 14, 1949), p. 46.

> Mrs. H- left on Friday for Regina where she will be looking after her grandchildren while her son Bill and wife attend a convention at Las Vegas, Nevada.

In the district reports one can read about what the children of residents are doing:

> J-P-, son of Mrs. P-P-, has been promoted from assistant postmaster at Nelson, B.C. to postmaster at Rossland, B.C.

People who have moved from the region are still able to maintain contact by reading the paper:

> I just love reading my hometown paper every week. ... We have been living in Montreal for six years now, and my husband H- is Assistant Superintendent with the Bank of Montreal, Head Office. Our eldest son, J-, is in second year McGill, and T- is in High School. ... If you have another copy of the News ... please send it to me as I often send the copies on to J-J- (née W-) in Moose Jaw.

The paper is local in orientation, taking little cognizance of wider issues. Judged by cosmopolitan standards, it is bland fare and of interest only if one knows the players. However, in this sparsely populated region one *does* know them.

Social Control

The constant talk and speculation about others effectively eliminates social and geographical space. Furthermore, it creates a distinctive social context with consequences for family relationships both within and outside the household. These emerge in the areas of social control, the institutionalization of values, and the patterning of social relationships.

This mechanism of social control has a striking effect upon children. From early in life, the child is aware of a network of kinsmen and nonkinsmen who assume responsibility for what they consider proper decorum. The concern with the child's ability to "behave" is not only made explicit to the child, but is also an issue of constant communication with the child's parents. The information is rarely neutral; rather, embedded in it are judgements about the child and his parents and how they meet the expectations of others.

Most commonly the chain of communication is from either of the child's grandmothers to his mother. The older woman calls daily to share information and to "see how things are". The older woman may inform the younger woman about a specific incident which she need not have witnessed. For example, after a ritual hello she will wait a short period and then mention that either she saw or heard that K- (the eight-year-old) was "downtown" yesterday. She will pause, and then say, "he was riding bicycles with J-. You have to talk to him. He and J- were up and down on the sidewalk and almost ran Mrs. P- down." Mrs. P- may have communicated through an intermediary, who transmitted the information to the grandmother, who in turn relayed it to the mother.

Instruction or opinion on how to discipline children is an area for common discussion. "Difficult" children – children who are hard to control – are well known and friends of the mother will conclude among themselves that it was "good" that K- was spanked the other day in the store because he was "getting out of hand". They might inform the mother later that her action was a wise one, thus reinforcing the mother when she performs in accordance with the accepted norms. Of course, the mother is criticized if she doesn't follow the accepted patterns of behaviour and it takes a hardy soul to withstand the social pressure and assume an independent position.

The extended kin group functions as an important social control agent throughout the lifetime of each member.[8] Proximity in social space can lead to the development of mechanisms for softening the impact of criticism. As one informant said:

> Sure everything is known by everybody, and you learn to live with it and not pay it any attention. . . . After all, if you let it bother you, it will drive you crazy.

As an adult, one learns to adapt and modify one's behaviour in accordance with these constraints.

It is during adolescence and early adulthood that the young person explicitly attempts to limit the social controls upon him by complaining about the community gossips and the lack of privacy. Since the adolescent's peers are in the same situation, the peer group offers empathy as well as support for the defiance of norms. Thus four or five girls as a group will perform public acts of bravado by, for example, appearing together downtown in miniskirts or short shorts. (This example comes from the early 1960s; in the early 1970s bravado was expressed by not wearing bras.) The fact that these actions are taken in concert dilutes the community opprobrium and gives the young people support in their attempts to gain independence from the social controls under which they have operated since childhood. Special occasions – such as graduation parties when everyone stays out all night, or showers for the groom where young men get drunk – also serve this function.

---

[8] Bernard Farber concludes that a major function of the kin group is to provide criticism and controls upon each nuclear unit. See *idem, Family Organization and Interaction* (San Francisco: Chandler Publishing Co., 1964). Thus the more important the kin group in the members' social lives, the more control can be exerted.

The fact that the older generation has passed through similar phases and "settled down" mitigates adult anxiety and criticism. Of course, since the adults' past misbehaviours are well known, their disapproval of the younger generation's misbehaviour leads to charges of hypocrisy.

Nevertheless, within the region an attempt is made to avoid judging others. There is a regional posture of high adaptive tolerance and avoidance of open controversy. Some quotes from interviews are illustrative:

> Personally I don't like A- but you have to give a man his due ... and he is a fine farmer.

> We neighbour some with ranchers. Ranchers now treat you just as good as another rancher. Of course, the differences are there but we don't talk about them any more ... at least not to each other.

> When they held the high school graduation they had only eight to graduate. I hear it's because so many of them have to get married when they're pregnant, but I haven't heard any of the women in the Ladies Club discuss it.

They believe in and practice the frontier code of "live and let live". Thus, although there is disapproval of illegitimacy, alcoholism, and extramarital relationships, that disapproval is not expressed openly and the individuals involved are not excluded from social affairs. Open confrontation occurs only under great stress or drunkenness, and both situations carry their own excuses. If the individual follows the other rules, the transgression (although never forgotten) is not held against him.

In part, the existence of a posture of high adaptive tolerance may be attributed to the frontier traditions of personal privacy and tolerance of individual difference – "so long as a man did his job".[9] However, the value placed on tolerance for the individual is also a particular adaptive strategy – a practical adjustment to a social situation in which there are few social alternatives and where all are subject to criticism. It is important to know how to "manage" oneself – to ignore the criticism – and to "manage" one's neighbours and kinsmen by making complaints about others indirectly, relying on the information network to get the message through.

This adjustment to interpersonal relationships where there is little opportunity for separation of roles is similar to that found in other face-to-face groups. Thus Frankenberg[10] found in his studies of a Welsh vil-

---

[9] L. Atherton, *The Cattle Kings* (Bloomington: Indiana University Press, 1961). Also, J. MacGregor recalls, "In those early days ... who could tell what history lay behind his neighbour? No one probed too deeply. You could never tell about the early pioneers in Western Canada." See *idem, Northwest of Sixteen* (Rutland, Vermont: Charles E. Tuttle Co., 1968), pp. 92-93.

[10] *Op. cit.*, pp. 270-272.

lage that differences of opinion did not become open, but rather were fought out through gossip and scandal, so that many of the villagers who were hostile could still maintain outward relations of harmony and friendship. This would seem to be a common and effective means of handling one's vulnerability to others where all of one's activities involve the same group. Conflicting groups must remain in physical proximity, so conflicts must somehow be resolved and open disputes avoided.

This pattern of interaction is continued within the agricultural household and is particularly evident in the relationship between father and son. The fact that there are few occupational alternatives and that the son is dependent upon his father to enter the occupation requires he accede to his father's demands and authority. As one young man put it: "...a man is stuck with his father ... he knows he is with him for life, and the only way to get along is not to complain or argue too much." Sons who may even desire to farm, but who are unable to manage the conflict between their desires for autonomy and the acceptance of authority, simply leave the family and enterprise. They may work for others in agriculture or in construction, using the skills they have acquired while growing up. The time spent away permits a cooling of emotions. While all who leave do not return home (see Chapter VI), those who do, return with a financial stake sufficient either to permit their starting out on their own place (with additional family help) or to become manager of the family farm after the father is ready to retire.

Another means of releasing hostility but avoiding open confrontation is through the use of jokes and teasing. The ability to "take a joke" and not take offense is part of how others judge you. There is a great deal of parent- or adult-child and male-female interaction which consists of teasing. Loudon[11] reports on the various contexts and contents of teasing behaviour among the islanders of Tristan da Cunha. He sees teasing as a means of raising children to be obedient as well as an important factor in releasing aggression and hostility in a personalistic and egalitarian social system. Similar behaviour exists in Jasper among peers and between men and women. However, in Jasper the teasing of children by adults is a manifestation of affection as well as an inducement to docility. (This is discussed at greater length in Chapter V.)

The lack of social and economic alternatives, the pressures of conformity, and the generalized style of handling conflict indirectly in order to avoid what the community calls "rocking the boat" would certainly encourage character traits of cautiousness and patience in contrast with innovativeness and spontaneity.

---

[11] J. B. Loudon, "Teasing and Socialization on Tristan da Cunha," in Philip Mayer, ed., *Socialization: The Approach from Social Anthropology* (London: Tavistock Publications, 1970), pp. 293-332.

Members of the region note that there are character traits which lend themselves to farming (and although not mentioned in this context, from an observer viewpoint they are also important for ranchers). In contrast with the romanticization of the rancher as "cowboy", men who stay and farm are viewed as having a certain type of personality: quiet, stable, and hardworking. Those young men who leave are defined as "live wires" or "restless":

> We have a son in the Air Force, but he'll never come home to the farm. He's too restless. He'd never contain himself on a farm because he likes the company of men and being busy all the time. He'd never be able to adapt himself to farm life again; he'd be bored....
>
> It's circumstance that says who stays on the farm and who goes somewhere else to do other work. Or sometimes it's the restless ones who leave. There's no glamour or excitement in a small town.

There is no analogous commentary regarding either the young women who marry and stay within the region or those who leave. Either decision can be made by "live wires" or quiet conformists. In the former case, an early marriage can be looked upon as a "solution", since marriage is one approved and early way for the young woman to get away from a restraining family situation.

The processes which define Jasper as a "friendly place" and a "good" place to live are the same processes which place constraints upon individuals.[12] For the Jasperite, neighbourliness – or, as it is used in Jasper, "neighbouring" – is more than "friendliness". It is inevitably more, since the individuals involved touch each other in several ways, through kinship and work associations as well as through friendship. These relationships involve important instrumental exchanges which include labour, machinery, time, advice, and so on. "Friendliness" or concern for others and its associated behaviours involve assuming responsibility for others – another manifestation of a set of ties that binds members of a community together.

There is no doubt that much of Jasper social life places constraints upon individuals. There is a routine to life; it is predictable with few surprises – "dull". However, all social situations carry within them differential distributions of costs and rewards. Jasper is no exception,

---

[12] Jasperites become well aware of these trade-offs early in life. A series of essays written at our request by fifteen- and sixteen-year-old high school students compared places to live. Although they overwhelmingly recognized the disadvantages of rural or small town life ("in a small town any misbehaviour is made known and spread over town"), they preferred it, viewing social life in cities as impersonal and distasteful:

"To live in such a city as Vancouver people are not as free. People in the city see so many different people from day to day that they hardly even know their own neighbours. From seeing so many people a person doesn't take as much an interest in the different personalities like we do in the rural areas where people are scarce...."

and those who find the costs too great leave.[13] This is not to say that there are no costs in leaving. These costs are often perceived most clearly by the out-migrant only after he has experienced life in the city. One common result is that the out-migrant who returns does so with a firm conviction that, whatever its shortcomings, Jasper is a better place to live than the city. This kind of selective out-migration reinforces the traditional patterns of interaction and maintains the social and cultural homogeneity of the region.[14]

[13] This is not to say that all those in pain can leave.

[14] Julian Steward makes a distinction between community stability and cultural stability. He writes that community stability or nonstability is commonly judged in terms of economic sufficiency and population movement (together with factors such as associational groupings). Depopulation is commonly considered as a criterion of instability although "it may bolster cultural conservation, for it is often the more acculturated persons, those who are assimilated in greater degree to the national culture who leave the community." See *idem, Area Research: Theory and Practice* (Social Science Research Council Bulletin 63, 1950), p. 42.

CHAPTER V

The Individual Life Cycle: A Participant in the Family Enterprise

When we examine the life cycle of the individual and the accompanying sets of expectations, it is important to remember that they do not cover the totality of rights and obligations available to people in any society. Further, it is also useful to recall that for the most part the stages themselves are gradual and overlapping, and are not necessarily consistent. Thus at age eighteen a woman is "adult" and may be responsible for a child, but in many areas she is not considered "adult" in terms of her responsibility to purchase alcoholic beverages.

In Jasper, as in all societies, the individual life cycle includes both biological (maturational) changes as well as certain cultural expectations. While Jasper agriculturalists, along with other North Americans, hold certain ideas as to the rights and obligations of young and old, male and female, the structural situation – that of family-owned and -operated resources – creates some specialized concepts. For example, we find that the demands the enterprise makes upon the family household for labour requires different ideas about the competence of children as compared with urban or suburban concepts. As one mother said:

> R- started helping his father about two years ago (at age 13). Before that he didn't do very much. He did learn to drive the garden tractor at about nine years and do that for me. I don't like to see him on top of all that machinery. I don't think any of the mothers do, but the fathers all think they should and push them. Right now he's doing a man's job (summer fallowing). But you have to let them — you can't get good hired help and anyway, I would rather not have them (the hired help) around.

Social expectations for age and sex are reflections of the larger social system. These expectations, which vary from society to society and also within societies, must be learned, and in doing so the child incorporates cultural rules and norms of behaviour.

Infancy and Childhood

The sex-neutral terminology used for male and female stages in Jasper is the same as that commonly used throughout North America: infant, toddler, preschool child, schoolchild, adolescent or teenager, young adult, adult, aged or old person.

Although stages of infancy and childhood are publicly defined as sexless (at least in the middle segments of the social structure), and there is no public acknowledgement or acceptance of sexual behaviour until the stage of "teenager", parents and other people involved in the socialization of the child are concerned that their children follow "proper" behaviour patterns for the sexes at each stage in the life cycle.

There is a generalized set of expectations for the individual's sex role which derives from the uteral stage, since it is believed that male foetuses will be more active (kick and push more) than female. These expectations concerning muscular activity continue through childhood and into adulthood: girls are expected to be quiet and prefer the house and household activities. Those girls who like the "outside" (Jasper term for work on the enterprise rather than in the home) are talked about as being "just like a boy". However, unlike the boy who is less active than the community expects him to be, the girl's behaviour is not a cause for concern — it is accepted with tolerance and sometimes pride. Women who had grown up on local ranches and farms made a point of describing their work:

> I always enjoyed the outside. . . . I helped with the branding and could just as well have been a boy. I wished I had been one. The other girls (her sisters) didn't help outside much but I helped Dad in everything.

Another woman, in her seventies, said with pride:

> Dad didn't have anyone to help him but us girls (there were three daughters) and we did everything.

Introspective, bookish, or domestically inclined boys are a source of real concern, since such behaviour is considered "sissyish". Parents want their sons to be "regular", that is, if a boy plays with girls or dolls or avoids the outdoors, there is fear that he will be a homosexual. Thus one mother, concerned that the six-year-old enjoyed watching "The Galloping Gourmet" on television, said:

> J- would rather watch that ["The Galloping Gourmet"] and cook than be outside ... we just hope he will come out of it.

This kind of behaviour is discussed by members of the kinship and social networks and the child is watched carefully for signs that he is "growing out of it", with each newly learned behaviour or skill checked for "maleness". Thus when this youngster began to play hockey, his kinsmen delighted in the fact.

Boys are expected to be "rough", unconcerned with protecting their bodies or their clothes; girls are expected to be the opposite. Boys should be "able to take it" (not cry or whine), behaviour which, while not encouraged for girls, is more acceptable for them. For boys, crying or complaining over hardship leads to accusations of their failure to be a boy; for a girl to cry or complain over hardship leads to accusations of her failure to be "big" or grown up.

During the period of childhood, the schools make no formal role distinction between boys and girls, and both sexes really occupy the same age-grade of "childhood" – nonetheless they live sexually segregated lives. With few exceptions boys are more rigid in maintaining their sexual boundaries than girls, and peers serve as severe critics if any boy dares to step across the sexual boundary. On the other hand, just as there is less adult opprobrium for the active girl than for the "sissy", girls are less concerned with maintaining sexual segregation and not infrequently search out boys for companionship and play. Similarly, boys will object to certain home tasks on the grounds that they are "girls' jobs", whereas girls can reach out into the work of the enterprise without censure. The greater number of acceptable alternatives for young girls remains as they mature, although they are still excluded from the primary agricultural occupational role of enterprise operator. (The ramifications of this exclusion are discussed in Chapter VII.)

Adolescence and Young Adulthood

With the onset of puberty, boy-girl relationships are now seen overtly in terms of their sexual behaviour. Since Jasper sexual ideology is the familiar double standard which permits sexual relationships outside of marriage for men (and in some situations encourages them) and prohibits them for women, girls are expected to learn to manage their sexual image so that they present one of limited availability. Where they are unable to do so, the goal of marriage is placed in jeopardy, since the girl has become sexually promiscuous or "the kind of girl you don't marry". Thus there is constant tension involved in boy-girl relationships in terms of the sexual availability or nonavailability of the girl.

There is widespread covert acceptance of the idea that sexual relationships are permissible before marriage for couples who are committed in some way towards one another, as in "going steady" or being engaged.[1] As a consequence, continual dating of the same person leads to the assumption by others in the community that the pair may be sexually involved and considering marriage. Both adolescent boys and girls complain that because of this they cannot have a friend of the opposite sex (by the term "friend" they mean a platonic relationship). Friendship is made difficult, since assumptions about marriage will be made which the young couple are not prepared to consider. The linking of sexual relationships and marriage and the circumscription of male-female relationships into one pattern of marriage are common phenomena which have only recently changed for some segments of the North American population.[2]

Although not as restricted as the young Irishmen in their twenties and thirties who Humphreys[3] reports avoided girls until they were financially able to marry, it is not unusual in Jasper for those young people who have goals which involve delaying marriage (for example, careers which require a college degree, or a desire to travel before "settling down") to monitor their number of dates and not date anyone consistently. As one mother said about her adolescent son who was planning to be a doctor:

> J- really likes M-, but he's afraid to date her.... People would start talking and he's just not ready for any serious relationship ... and neither is she. This way, they eye one another, and enjoy meeting one another at social affairs, but he won't ask her out.

Occasionally, one does observe male-female friendships in Jasper based on a fraternal model. These cases are acceptable. A young woman establishes a friendship with her boyfriend's or spouse's male friends, since it is assumed that loyalty to one's friends precludes sexual relationships with the friend's girl or spouse. However, elements of sexual tension *are* present in these situations.

---

[1] This is similar to the findings of Ira L. Reiss, *The Social Context of Pre-Marital Sexual Permissiveness* (New York: Holt, Rinehart and Winston, 1967).

[2] Robert O. Blood, *The Family* (New York: The Free Press, 1972), p. 319.

[3] Alexander J. Humphreys, *New Dubliners: Urbanization and the Irish Family* (New York: Fordham University Press, 1966), p. 174.

Daughters and Sons

Girls learn from early childhood that ranching or farming is considered a male occupation. Women can participate fully in the operation of the enterprise and their participation is economically important, particularly in families without sons. However, marriage is regarded as the ideal feminine career and women are not expected to operate a ranch or farm. With few exceptions, the only way a girl can hope to participate in the operation of an enterprise is through marriage to a rancher or farmer.

There were, during the decade of study, four women who did operate agricultural enterprises. As operators, they were considered to be "as good or better a worker than a man ... but they *look* like it," the implication being a negative one. However, attitudes are changing on feminine roles within this rural region as they are throughout North America. Where in interviews in 1963 and 1964 the issue of women taking control of the enterprise was generally disapproved – not wrong, but "just not done" – in 1971 we found at least one recent twelfth-grade graduate remaining home and working for her father for wages with little if any social comment. However, as yet she remains unique, and working for wages does not mean eventual succession.

The fact that expectations for the young woman's career are not bound up with the development of the enterprise makes it easier for her to leave in contrast with her brother. Girls not married after twelfth grade migrate out of the region and train in one or another of the service skills – teaching, nursing, or secretarial work – while retaining the eventual goal of marriage. These are skills about which the girls have direct knowledge, since there has been a consistent flow of trained women into the region. Fifty percent of the wives of agricultural operators in our regional sample worked prior to their marriage. Of these, 37 percent were teachers, 27 percent had secretarial or bookkeeping training, and 11 percent were nurses.

There are higher education expectations for daughters than for sons, as well as differential rates in fulfillment of these expectations. Daughters, ranch or farm, do better in school than do sons: 79 percent of the farm girls and 70 percent of the ranch girls finished twelfth grade and up as compared with 69 percent of the farm sons and 27 percent of the ranch sons.[4]

---

[4] Hall and McFarland find a similar situation. They conclude that "... the school world of Paulend and Croyden (pseudonyms) turns out to be, fundamentally, an academic atmosphere in which girls thrive and boys fail. ... Moreover, the school is a feminine world in the vocational sense. It prepares them admirably for their careers in the work world. The skills they learn are immediately transferable to the job world. Especially is this true for those who continue to university, those who prepare for school teaching and nursing, and those who enter clerical occupations. ... The gra-

Two important life-cycle ceremonials: marriage and a birthday celebration.

Parents, particularly mothers, project onto the girl the urban middle-class ideals of what is proper in terms of achievement and decorum. Ranch or farm wives would find that their social life differed from that of urban or suburban women mostly in minor ways. The overriding concern of women in both social settings with family, home, and husband tends to one of patterning their lives in similar ways despite the fact that the communities in which they live are differently organized. It is this uniformity in the women's roles and experiences transmitted by mothers to daughters which enables the rural girl to prepare more successfully than her brother for life in urban settings.

In contrast with the expectations held for young women – marriage or migration from the region – the expectations held for the young man keep him within the family. A young man raised in a family agricultural enterprise has an option open to relatively few other young adults: he can receive formal acknowledgement by the community with regard to his adult status and still remain within the family household. Unlike the urban child, he is not pushed out of the family, but is, in addition, generally encouraged to remain by the positive value the community places on continuity of the family name in the particular enterprise. However, along with the option and pressure to remain in the family and enterprise are his own desires for autonomy, deriving from the general individualism of the culture and social system.

Throughout childhood, the son works under the direction of his father, the boss of the enterprise. The relationship between father and son, therefore, has many of the features of the relationship between employer and hired hand. The work activities follow a pattern in which the father assumes the direction and planning and performs the lighter jobs, while the son follows orders and does the heavier work. In a task like fence building, the father chooses the location, tamps the dirt, and the son pounds the posts into the ground and stretches the wire. When the son gets older and his experience accumulates, he is ready to assume the direction of the tasks and the enterprise as a whole. However, since the father is less able to perform the heavy work and yet does not wish to relinquish control, the son becomes more of a labourer despite his readiness to assume administrative responsibility.

The participation of the son on the enterprise involves him in the world of men. There is little age or class segregation. A stranger watching a work crew would have difficulty knowing who was owner, owner's son, or hired labourer. There is an egalitarian code which demands that the hired hand be housed, fed, and treated as part of the family. More-

---

duate of a stenography course can start work immediately as a full-fledged stenographer. The graduate of a four-year course in mechanics starts as an apprentice." See Oswald Hall and Bruce McFarland, *Transition from School to Work* (Department of Labour Report No. 10, Canada, 1962), p. 65.

over, the work process itself, with its necessity for all men to cooperate on specific tasks with relatively equal skills, is one which serves as a base for, and reinforcer of, egalitarian values.

The young son's friends are the local hired hands (who not uncommonly are distant relatives or the sons of friends or neighbours) who, due to conflict with their own fathers or because there are too many brothers and not enough land, have left their own home to work for someone else. These friendship groups of young men are important socializing agents and serve to introduce the young son into male role behaviour involving women, drinking, and work. They are also important for social support since they essentially share the same position *vis-à-vis* their fathers. They drink, go to dances together and look for women, and complain to one another about their respective situations as well as provide important sources of labour for work exchange. These friendships reinforced by work parallel – although they do not replicate – the work exchange and friendship groups of the older generation.

Adulthood

Marriage for both young men and women signifies adulthood. In contrast to the son, whose marriage entails new financial and social adjustments, marriage of the daughter can be viewed as a solution to several problems for the agricultural family household.[5] Before her marriage, there is likely to be a certain amount of conflict with her parents over a large variety of things: work, school, dress, hair, sex, future, and friends.

Marriage of the daughter, particularly where the young husband is approved of and has some financial security or opportunity, is always encouraged. Such a marriage can be viewed in terms of transferring to the new husband the consumption needs of the daughter and freeing the household of the obligation to support her. Marriage frees the family from the moral responsibility to limit the sexual availability of the adolescent girl, and it also diminishes the potential rivalry between mother and daughter in relation to the husband/father.

Marriage of the son, unlike that of the daughter, creates a fresh set of problems, since a new household is established, placing additional

---

[5] Bohannon suggests that in North America marriage is a solution for the strains upon the young person resulting from the cultural pressures for independence from his parents. One's spouse assumes a "parenting" (his term) role as well as solving the issue of sexuality. I have no disagreement with his formulation; however, the point I would like to emphasize is that since the son's occupational opportunity is connected to his continuing relationship with his father, his early marriage does not provide the same degree of solution as does that of the daughter. Paul Bohannon, "Dyad Dominance and Household Maintenance," in Francis Hsu, ed., *Kinship and Culture* (Chicago: Aldine Press, 1971), p. 60.

consumption demands on the enterprise. Although the ideal has always been to have one's own place independent of the family, nevertheless, in all of the marriages between 1956 and 1970 in the sample population where the male immediately associated himself with his father's enterprise, 18 percent of the young couples lived at least briefly with the male's parents. Even where the young couple does not share the same household or live on the same enterprise, they do expect to be linked to their parents' activities and expect their parents to be involved in theirs. The young man continues to work with his father, taking lunch breaks and dinner with his mother. The young wife is similarly involved in the shared household activities and, if she so desires, in the enterprise activities. The following quote from a newly married woman is illustrative:

> I'm lucky to be in the ideal situation (in a mobile home next to her in-laws' house) where I'm not limited by there just being the two of us, for I can always send our surplus (dinner) to J-'s family or have them all in to help us clean up what I've made. It really couldn't be better.

The phase of "young married" in Jasper, with its emphasis on the conjugal relationship and with its comparatively less sexually segregated social life, is a brief one. Jasper male-female relationships are similar to, although perhaps not as totally segregated as, those Frankenberg reports for Glynceiriog (Wales):

> [I] suggest, with some exaggeration but much truth, that except for a brief period of courtship and early marriage, there seem to be two villages, one of men and one of women, which rarely mingle.[6]

Both ranch and farm men have strong peer group relationships which are implemented in daily tasks: the trip to town to repair machinery becomes a social occasion, including gossip sessions at the restaurant or beer parlour or on the street. Men utilize work occasions as social opprotunities, although this is more common among the ranchers due to the greater need for group labour than on the more mechanized farms, and it was more common in the past than it is today. Nevertheless, the work situation continues to be combined with social activities and, as such, excludes women whose primary tasks are within the home. Similarly, the social opportunities for women based upon the woman's world of home, club, and kin largely exclude men. Through their separate social and work activities, men and women establish independent ties with others. However, due to the limited number of alternatives, these ties are complementary and they incorporate (for the most part) different members of the same household.

---

[6] Frankenberg, *op. cit.*, p. 92.

Helen Lopata[7] summarizes types of companionate relations of married couples in the following categories:

1. Sex-segregated friendship relations in which both husband and wife participate in different groups.
2. Sex-segregated friendship relations in which the *husband* has a close friend or is attached to a clique while the wife is relatively isolated.
3. Sex-segregated friendship relations in which the *wife* has a close friend or is attached to a clique without a parallel involvement by the husband.
4. Sex-segregated friendship relations entirely connected with the male kin line.
5. Couple-only companionate relations in which the husband and wife lack any sex-segregated friendships, engaging only in leisure activities as couples.
6. Couple-plus, sex-segregated companionate relations include both couple socializing and peer friendship developed by each partner.

The position of the young wife who is a newcomer to the region falls in the second category of Lopata's scheme: she is an outsider, whereas her husband is able to maintain his past ties. However, over time this changes to friendships based upon couple socializing as well as independent friendships (Lopata's sixth category). During the first years of her marriage, the young wife who comes from outside the region is socially dependent upon her husband and his mother and other female kinsmen for her incorporation into the social life of the community. She is expected by her in-laws to assume social ties similar to those held by her mother-in-law or sister-in-law. She accompanies them to the organizational meetings in which they participate, slowly evolving for herself a set of friends. Where ideas about community participation differ between daughter-in-law and mother-in-law, the differences can lead to conflict between them. This is just one aspect of the process of developing acceptable concepts of obligations and rights in the mother-in-law/daughter-in-law relationship. As one woman said:

> There were two things I had to work out with my mother-in-law. The first was that H- (husband) didn't have to eat dinner at her house every noon. The second was that I didn't have to go with her when she went to the Ladies Aid meetings.

Or, as another woman noted:

> A- (friend and ranch wife) never goes into town and never has joined any of the clubs. M- (A-'s mother-in-law and active club woman) never got over this and still can't understand why....

[7] Helen Lopata, *Occupation: Housewife* (Oxford: Oxford University Press, 1971), pp. 304-306.

The young woman's friendships need not necessarily parallel her husband's work relationships or kin networks. This was more likely to be true in the past, when the opportunities for the woman to leave the home were more limited than they are today; she now has access to the car. Her friendships are based upon similar situational factors: for example, the age of the children, her degree of mobility, the degree of her incorporation into the day-to-day operation of the enterprise and, of course, personality factors. The point, however, is that her friendships are external to the enterprise and may or may not be located within the larger kin unit. Where kin and enterprise and friendships of the young wife coincide, there is less sexual and work segregation between men and women, and between family social activities and enterprise work activities. The one reinforces the other. Even where they do not mesh, the small scope for friendships does not permit sex-segregated relations which are completely isolated from one another's friendship circles.

Married couples are supposed to have children soon after marriage, and 48 percent of the children born in 1935 or later were born within the first year of marriage. Few marriages were without children. (.05 percent, in fact). Children are desired and seen as "natural" components of the totality of one's life.[8] Contraception is practised and, for the most part, the ideal number of children desired conforms closely to the actual number born.[9]

With the birth of children, the wife's role (*vis-à-vis* the husband) is diminished and her role of mother (*vis-à-vis* the child) becomes critical. "Mother" defines for the woman her dominant social relationships *vis-à-vis* family and community (see Chapter V).

When the children reach school age, the young woman begins to participate actively in community organizations. The family usually joins a church so that the children can go to Sunday school; they generally participate in 4H activities along with the children. As the children mature, the woman's participation in activities outside the home changes, as does her husband's. The husband has assumed greater responsibility for the operation of the enterprise; generally, by this time, his father has retired and the *total* responsibility for the enterprise is the younger man's. Both husband and wife have diverse demands made on their time which makes for increased sexual segregation with increased length of marriage.[10]

---

[8] This is similar to the desires of a sample of University of Saskatchewan students. See S. Parvez Wakil, "Campus Mate Selection Preferences: A Cross-National Comparison," *Social Forces,* 51 (1973), 474.

[9] The mean number of children present in households in 1962 was 2.4; 2.6 in 1972. The mean number of children born to the sample population of operators and their wives was 3.0 in 1962 and 3.2 in 1972.

[10] This is similar to the findings reported in Blood, *op. cit.,* p. 428.

At this time, daughters and mothers resume a closeness lost during adolescence and the early years of marriage.[11] The daughter has experienced the same problems adjusting to her situation as did her mother. She shares with her mother similar experiences in child rearing, despite frequent disagreements about child-rearing practices. Further, mothers (grandmothers) offer important emotional and economic support during the early years of child rearing which the daughter (new mother) is now able to accept. They find companionship in one another, shop, visit, and vacation together. It is the mother who reintroduces her daughter into the social and community organizations.

As the children mature, the woman's participation in the work of the enterprise is less necessary. Usually she will do more work in the house, although she still remains an important part of the enterprise in contrast with her urban counterpart who is isolated from her husband's place of work. It is a rare woman who maintains her active participation in the fields as she ages. In part this change is due to fewer needs for manual labour – there are now children of an age who can help; in part it is due to the particular stage in the development of the enterprise – the early period required more labour on the part of every member of the family. Thus, as the family matures and the enterprise develops, the woman is increasingly occupied in the house, and it is at this time that she will exert pressure on her husband to fix it up, redecorate, or pay for a remodelling job.

This is also the period when the mature woman can, if she so desires, take a greater part in social activities within the community which may not be directly tied to her children's needs. The older women whose children are of high school age or older are the most active participants and leaders in the clubs and church organizations in both town and country. Such participation in community organizations reinforces the mature woman's ties to the regional culture, which she communicates to other members of her family.

The mature man ideally has assumed control of the enterprise and has, over the years, developed its resources to a point we have called the "maintaining" stage. His work, social and kinship ties are multiple ones; and economically, if he so desires, he is able to consider alternatives other than the development of the enterprise. For some, the primary focus remains the continued expansion and development of the enterprise. We have termed these men "enterprise-oriented". For others, the focus changes from the development of the enterprise to participation within the community, often into fields divorced from agriculture: town lodges, sports, politics. There is a convergence of economic maturity and biosocial development which permits the interests of the man to diverge from a total concern with his chief occupation.

---

[11] Similar findings are reported in Michael Young and Peter Willmott, *Family and Kinship in East London* (Glencoe, Illinois: The Free Press, 1957).

Aging

For women, the process of aging does not seem to be as difficult as it is for men. Given the sexual code of the region, with its heavy investment in motherhood as contrasted with wifehood, the image of woman after a short period of marriage is not that of sexual object. Jasper women may appear to age more rapidly in physical appearance than middle-class urban women, yet they remain on a plateau of social activity for a longer period of time before becoming culturally "old". Unlike their male counterparts, they do not invest their lives in an enterprise which they must turn over to another younger person. Women invest their lives in their family, which ages along with them. As women age, they continue to participate in the same social and community organizations they always did – there is far less discontinuity in their lives than in that of their husbands.

Aging for the man involves much greater adjustment than for the woman in terms of the sense of self.[12] Retirement is a crisis, and most operators avoid it as long as possible. Since the role of the man is tied to the occupation, the transfer of control of resources from father to son involves "giving up" the self, the identity. The father has spent his life doing just one thing: building an enterprise. One woman, who had been discussing the question of her husband's retirement, said:

> I don't think we could turn the place over to J- and continue to live there (retire on the place while their son ran it).... We would have to move ... when you love something you can't turn it over to somebody and watch them doing things because in most instances they will not do them the way you would do them and this creates all kinds of problems....

Along with the attitudes acquired by individuals in a culture which does not value age, the father is pressured by the younger man to give up the very activity which defines him as a social person: he is asked to surrender his life's work to an uncertain future. From this perspective it is understandable why there are few formal father-son succession agreements.

Most commonly, if a man is not being pushed out by a son who is desirous to take over the enterprise he will "stay on", "cutting down" his work but not actually retiring. Most of those men who do formally retire never quite manage to "let go", and as an informant stated, "the old man is always out here to see what's going on".

---

[12] Yonina Talmon's studies of aging in collective settlements in Israel indicate that women have a more difficult time than men. See *idem,* "Aging in Israel, A Planned Society," in Bernice L. Neugarten, ed., *Middle Age and Aging* (Chicago: University of Chicago Press, 1968), pp. 461-468. She notes that Townsend records that in working-class families men have a more difficult time adjusting to aging than women. See Peter Townsend, *The Family Life of Old People* (New York: The Free Press of Glencoe, 1957).

Given the continuity of kinship and friendship networks, both men and women maintain their social ties after retirement by continuing to participate in the same organizations, and through social visiting patterns which after retirement increase both in number and duration.

This continuity can, however, present problems. In recent years, as families have retired to town,[13] they have managed to live near one another. Thus, there will be four or five families from one district living on the same street in Jasper. These past social ties carried into retirement were based upon significant instrumental exchanges, but in town, the instrumentality of the exchange is no longer an issue and, in some situations, old neighbours and friends find that the social ties cannot be maintained. This leads to personal hostilities between old friends.

The problems of getting old are mitigated by the fact that there is greater regard in Jasper for the accomplishment and contribution that the older man and his wife have made. The young couple is fully aware that without their parents' achievement of building an enterprise, their own life would have been very different — certainly more precarious — and there is recognition of a debt which can never be repaid.

---

[13] Sixty-eight percent of the operators who retired between 1962 and 1972 retired to Jasper; 21 percent remained on their enterprise or in their local village; 11 percent retired to Medicine Hat.

CHAPTER VI

Family Roles & Relationships

The Jasper agricultural family contains structural features common to all North American families. These include bilateral descent with its flexible institutional patterns of inheritance, rights, and obligations. A strong value is placed on neo-local residence and the nuclear family household.

Although household composition changes over time and can expand to include other members of the kin group as situational factors involving subsistence or residential needs develop — what has been called "growth potential"[1] — ,the nuclear family household remains the ideal, as well as the statistically dominant type of household structure. Table 8 presents the classificatory data on household composition in 1962 and 1972. As indicated, the majority of the households are composed of a married couple and their children, with very little difference

---

[1] W. Davenport, "Introduction", in S. Mintz and W. Davenport, eds., "Working Papers in Caribbean Social Organization", *Social and Economic Studies,* 10 (December 1961, a special number), 380-385.

between the two time periods. However, these data do not adequately reflect the brief sojourn of the young married couple in the parental home, a practice more common in the past. In fact, 43 percent of the agriculturalists operating an enterprise in 1962 had lived with either the husband's or wife's parents after marriage; by 1972, this percentage had dropped to 38 percent, and in the recent marriages (those between 1956 and 1970), only 18 percent of the couples moved in with parents after marriage. Today, when the prospective heir marries, he is more likely to live in a trailer next to his parents' home than he is to move into the same house with them. The young couple will live typically in the trailer until they can establish themselves on their own place or until the senior generation retires. During this phase the enterprise is classified as one composed of multiple households (see Table 9). While the tables of household composition are useful and important indicators of change, the more significant issue concerns the roles and relationships among the household members and their larger kin groups.

Husbands and Wives

There is general consensus as to the division of labour between husbands and wives as regards household tasks. The responsibility of the household as that of the woman's is justified situationally: "the wife cooks because she is home and I am in the field". The image of the ideal woman is that of the frontier woman who "does what has to be done", but, aside from this vague prescription which takes for granted the woman's household tasks, there is flexibility in the role which the farm or ranch wife can play in the enterprise. The economic hardships of the frontier period and that of the depression, reinforced the dual sets of expectations for woman in both the public and private spheres. No matter the home responsibilities, women were also important labour resources in the building of the enterprise. This duality continues today, a consequence of the interrelationship of family household and family enterprise. However, the fact that household tasks are taken for granted as women's responsibilities and not shared responsibilities of both husband and wife, means that any other tasks which the woman assumes are added on to her original work load in the household. (Herein lies the basis for the woman's "double burden".)

The rigid division of labour within the house between husband and wife does not mean there is no interaction and companionship between the spouses. The proximity of work and residence and the fact that the enterprise is also the family household of necessity involve the woman in the work world of men, although not vice versa. (This is a continuation of the childhood social patterns which permit girls to seek out boys for play but not vice versa.)

Women's participation spans virtually the entire range of enterprise activities. Her participation in the enterprise varies according to her own desires and values, the needs of the enterprise, and the expectations of her husband and other members of the family enterprise. Women ride in roundups, bale hay, keep the books, participate in the continual task of fencing, put out salt in the summer, and so on. Few women do all these things and some women do none of them, but the fact is that women feel free to participate in the life of the enterprise in a variety of ways. There seems to be little overt community social pressure for or against this kind of activity as long as the woman adequately fulfills what is considered her primary responsibility as wife and mother.

In contrast with the variability of women's activities in community and enterprise, there is greater specificity for men. There is a less diffuse concept of what defines "manliness". There is an agreed-upon image of the man which incorporates the mass symbols of the cowboy and the West. People talk about it as a "Zane Grey" image. The more specialized and less diffuse expectations for men can also be found in the shared agreement that a man's occupation is to be found in active work in the outdoors in ranching or farming and the subsequent high proportion of succession by sons to the family enterprise. Men also report they "feel" community judgment regarding their activities on the enterprise. Although women do not report similar community pressures as to enterprise activities, there are, however, pressures within the family with which the young wife must cope.

The young wife enters a situation where her husband has been used to a particular style of social participation established by his mother. For example, where the mother has had both the energy and organizational ability to participate vigorously in enterprise affairs, and where the young wife may not match this style, invidious comparison becomes inevitable. The difficult situation of the young wife is compounded by the fact that there are new recreational and social alternatives – such as more numerous women's clubs, curling and skiing – which were not available to her mother-in-law and are attractive to the wife without skills or incentives for enterprise activity. Conflicts which arise from this source can be resolved as the young wife matures and establishes her own style of participation in the enterprise.

As in all family situations, there is inevitable conflict and stress. One means of resolving conflict is divorce. However, among Jasper agriculturalists it is a relatively rare solution.[2] Other indicators of stress

---

[2] In our regional study sample there was only one case of divorce during the ten-year period of study. Some statistical data for the Census District population, of which our study sample is part, indicates that although divorced persons have slightly increased from 1966 to 1971, nevertheless they represent only a small proportion of individuals.

are neurotic and psychotic symptoms. Our mental health data indicate a population with relatively good social adjustment and, in general, a low referral rate for psychiatric treatment. Further, when we compare the 1961 referral rates for psychiatric treatment with those of 1971, we find that the rate of referral for women declines by 10 percent. In addition, there is a decline in the referral rate (14 percent) among farmers and stockraisers during the same period. The increased relative prosperity of the Jasper agriculturalist in this same period suggests a connection between the alleviation of some of the earlier hardships and the concomitant strains upon social relationships among family members.

The primary responsibility of the farm or ranch wife is that of cook and quartermaster. The men eat all meals at home, as well as "lunch", which is comparable to the urban coffee break. The wife is responsible for ensuring that there is always sufficient food to serve anyone who is there, and where there are hired hands, they also are served. With the help of a freezer – an appliance all households have since the introduction of electricity in the mid 1950s[3] – and the liberal use of potatoes and bread as staples in all meals, she manages nicely. Dinner is served at noon and is the major meal of the day. It is scheduled precisely and a woman must plan her day around her presence in the home between 11:30 and 1:30. If she cannot avoid being away, she makes other arrangements for the men to have dinner. Where there are two women and separate kitchens in multiple household enterprises, the responsibility is shared and dinner chores are alternated. The set time of dinner keeps the woman housebound and time conscious.

Women also must make special arrangements for social intercourse. While they utilize the shopping tour to town to meet and visit friends and family, they must watch the clock, since dinner must be served and children cared for. The round of their daily life is ordered by the clock and by the demand of others.

Unlike the male whose work changes according to the season, the woman's work remains the same throughout the year:

> There's always the kids, cooking and the house ... in winter we curl; in the summer I have a garden, but it's pretty much the same all year.

	Total Married Population		Total Widowed Population		Divorced Population	
	1966	1971	1966	1971	1966	1971
Male	3855	3575	236	205	18	40
Female	3775	3560	665	645	19	30
Total	7630	7135	901	850	37	70

Source: Census of Canada 1966, 1971.

[3] *The Report of the Royal Commission on the Status of Women in Canada* (Ottawa, 1970), p. 41, notes that in 1968 more than three times as great a percentage of farm as city households had home freezers.

Women's work, however, does change in terms of the family cycle because it is dependent upon the demands of the family which reflect the composition of the household and the ages of household members.

TABLE 8: Household Composition, 1962-1972

	1962		1972	
	No.	%	No.	%
Households composed of:				
Single Occupant	6	5	2	1
Unmarried Kinsmen (brothers, brother-sister, uncle-nephew, etc.	6	5	2	1
More than one occupant without Kin or Affinal Tie	2	2	0	0
Married Couple	19	15	35	25
Married Couple with Unmarried Children	83	65	93	67
Married Couple with Married Children	6	5	3	2
Married Couple with Non-Married Kinsmen	5	4	4	3
Total No. Households	127	101	139	99

TABLE 9: Enterprises Composed of Multiple and Single Households, 1962-1972

	1962				1972			
	Ranch		Farm		Ranch		Farm	
	No.	%	No.	%	No.	%	No.	%
Multiple Household Enterprises	10	31	14	18	12	43	13	20
Single Household Enterprises	22	69	64	82	16	57	52	80
Total	32	100	78	100	28	100	65	100

Women evolve patterns of participation in the enterprise activities, the consequences of which are discussed in the following chapter. However, no matter what their style of participation, women share a common means for controlling expectations with regard to the amount of work they do. They simply *do not learn* how to do certain things, a practice clearly articulated by women as the most effective means of handling the situation.

Mrs. S-, for example, never learned how to drive "... if I did, it would always be 'mother get this, mother get that.' I have enough to do." Again Mrs. D- never learned how to milk " ... if I did, then it would be my job forever – this way J- (her husband) does it." It is analogous to the male never learning how to cook or change a baby. It is not that one cannot do such work, or that it is not proper, but rather that each has enough to do without adding more.

The way one makes a decision not to participate or learn is a complex process. In no interview or conversation did a woman say that certain work was *not* "women's work". Explanations were idiosyncratic, or put in terms of happenstance, for example, "I just never did do that" or "my mother never did that and I don't see why I should."

The wife is responsible for the behaviour of the children; her husband for their labour and training and the success of the enterprise. Although the woman is dependent upon her husband for her status in the community, insofar as she shares the social credit he receives as a "good operator", she also has an independent position. This is based upon the prestige of her lineage and the community's perception of the "goodness" of her children, as well as her own "goodness" as housekeeper and quartermaster, helpful neighbour, and friend. The role the woman plays in controlling family expenditures and family consumption wants is important in the judgements of the community and the larger kin group. Her monitoring of family expenditures is important in the success or failure of the development process of the enterprise.

Many farmers and ranchers – perhaps a majority – are dependent upon wives for help in bookkeeping, letter writing, and dealing with bureaucratic agencies. In the past, as well as in the present period, women have had had a higher level of education than men (see Table 10).

TABLE 10: Educational Levels of Women and Men, 1962-1972

	Elem. No.	Elem. %	H.S. No.	H.S. %	H.S. Grad. No.	H.S. Grad. %	College No.	College %	Total No.	Total %
1962										
Wives	31	24	55	43	17	13	24	30	127	100
Operators	71	56	39	31	9	7	8	6	127	100
1972										
Wives	17	15	52	46	18	16	26	23	113	100
Operators	48	43	39	35	16	14	10	9	113	101

Men are also dependent upon their wives for social interaction outside of the work group. The woman organizes social relationships between the family as a household and the outside world. She establishes the social context of the household since, for example, she makes the decisions as to who shall or shall not be invited to dinner. By decisions of this type she establishes reciprocal ties with other members of the kin group and the larger community.

Parents and Children

Strong emphasis is placed upon the parent-child bond.[4] This emphasis does not mean that the bond between husband and wife is unimportant, that the woman does not receive status in terms of her role as wife, or that she does not meet the expectations of the wife's role. However, neither women nor men see their primary roles as wife and husband.[5]

Men classify themselves in terms of their occupation or, in the family, as father and son. While it is true that a woman is accorded status in terms of whom she marries, the emphasis on the role of a conjugal partner is important for only a few years of marriage. With the birth of children, the role of mother becomes critical. It defines woman's dominant social relationships *vis-à-vis* family and community just as occupation defines the man's roles – a common situation in modern society.[6]

There are issues of *age* and *generation* which are present in all parent-child relationships. The way parental power and authority is viewed in the parent-child transaction and the way parents pace their children through childhood are related to the view that parents hold of childhood and the expectations which they hold for their children. While families differ, there are certain expectations held for children which are widely shared.

Issues of Authority and Generation: Decorum

There was general agreement that children are expected to defer to adults; they are expected to be "good" – not to touch things and to sit quietly in company and at the dinner table. They are expected to learn to behave as adults in adult situations. An example from field notes taken in 1970 illustrates:

> The two-year-old was in her high chair and had finished her dinner. She wanted to get out. (There was a lot of company in the room and her older sister had left the table.) Her mother was talk-

---

[4] This emphasis is similar to what Hsu calls dominant dyads. Francis Hsu, "A Hypothesis on Kinship and Culture," in Francis Hsu, ed., *Kinship and Culture* (Chicago: Aldine Publishing Co., 1971), pp. 3-29.

[5] Also see Lopata, *op. cit.* p. 48.

[6] I suggest that this is the case since the conjugal role emphasizes a sexual relationship, whereas the mother-role de-emphasizes sex. The mother-focus, common to many working-class families, may be viewed as a way to "control" the women's sexuality, and may also "age" her and, given the tightly knit social networks, symbolically establish her non-availability to other men.

ing with one of the visitors and ignored the child's cries to get down. The child banged her dish on her tray, threw her spoon down and cried to her mother. Mother picked up spoon and bowl and spanked the child's hands, remarking to the visitor that X (child) was stubborn. Child cried quietly then climbed out of her chair herself. Mother picked child up, spanked her hard on the bottom and placed her back in the high chair, telling her she had to learn to wait until "mother was ready" and that she was a "naughty girl." Child cried loudly, and father intervened with a look and a raised hand and said, "stop making all that noise!" Child cried quietly. Mother talked with visitor about how she (the child) was stubborn, and that she had to learn. After a few minutes in which the child cried quietly, Grandmother took the child out of the chair and put her down saying, "Now you'll be a good girl."

Children are included in dinners, birthdays, and anniversary celebrations and parties and, until recently, dances.[7] Although they are incorporated in the adult social activities, they are expected to listen and not be heard. They are not expected to participate in the conversation, although they frequently serve as a focal topic. Stories are told about the child's transgression and how the child had to be punished. As long as he remains quiet – "good" – and does not interfere with the conversation, he may stay. The fact that children have learned to defer to adults means that adult social life can flow evenly in their presence.

Numerous writers on family and socialization have emphasized the difference in expectations for children's decorum in terms of class position: for example, the working class emphasizes obedience whereas the middle class is more concerned with self-control or self-direction.[8] Pearlin,[9] in his study of Turinese family life, notes that men who perceive that their jobs require a large measure of self-direction are more likely to value self-control for their children than men who do not. Men whose jobs require little or no self-direction are likely to value obedience. In Jasper agricultural families, adult demands for obedience by the child were commonly observed. However, when parents were asked the question, obedience was mentioned by only one family. Other responses emphasized the need for children to learn self-control and self-reliance. Typical of other responses were the following: learn to work and cooperate with one another; to be good citizens, respectful and honest; to have a sense of responsibility; to be sensible; to be considerate of others, capable of doing things.

---

[7] A decision to attend a dance "as a family" depends upon the type of music that will be played. Parents and children will attend together as a family where the music is "old time".

[8] M. L. Kohn, "Social class and Parent-child Relationships, "*American Journal of Sociology*, 68(1959),471-480.

[9] L. I. Pearlin, *Class-context and Family Relations: A Cross-National Study* (Boston: Little, Brown, 1971).

Farming is singularly demanding of those characteristics of self-reliance and self-direction, and the emphasis that parents place upon their children learning self-control supports Pearlin's hypothesis of the relationship between work and parental values. However, the fact that parents value the quality of self-control does not negate the importance they attach to their children exhibiting obedience and deference to adults.

Issues of Authority and Generation: Sanctions

All types of sanctions – both rewards and punishments – are used by adults to ensure and encourage desired behaviour. The former consists of incentives of consumption items, money, or additional privileges. The latter consists of withdrawal of privileges (for example, food), or physical punishment (spanking or whipping). In response to questions about the discipline of children, parents state that they attempt to "reason" with the child, or "explain". In no case will they say that the favoured punishment is physical. However, if our observations are correct, physical punishment is common. In fact, in public settings a father's raised hand is sufficient to produce the desired result.

There is little overt praise for the successful performance of a chore even where parental pleasure in the child's performance is obvious. The following example is from 1971 field notes:

> We were sitting and watching B- (the six-and-a-half-year-old son) mow the field. He was using a small power garden mower which one rides. W- (his mother) told us how pleased she was that he was finally showing an interest in the ranchwork. And that ever since this little mower came B- wanted to use it. "Last year his feet didn't even reach the pedals, but he is finally big enough." Today was the first time he had ever done so large an expanse of grass. Usually he only did the front part of the lawn. A short time later B- came into the living room, flushed and smiling. W- (his mother) said: "Have you finished? Did you do a good job? Did you get between the trees? ... you better wash up now."

The above comment by the mother was made with warmth and affection which indicated her pleasure even though there was no explicit praise.

There is much teasing and bantering between parents and children (also between men and women, older relatives and younger) which serves to communicate affection as well as an important socialization device. For example:

> Aunt to niece (said with a hug to the child): "who put your hair up in curlers? Did Grandma? You're a horror!"

> Grandfather to granddaughter: "Hi stinkypoops!" Granddaughter: "I'm not stinky." Grandfather (reaching out for child): "Come here, ugly ... what have you been doing today?"

> Father to assembled company in daughter's presence: "Cindy's O.K. – for someone with not much in the head department."

The absence of explicit verbal statements of affection and praise of children by adults is part of a general pattern of suppressed emotionalism common among both men and women. Even so, there is wide divergence between male and female in the degree of emotionalism which is considered proper to express. Women are expected to show emotion as long as it is not too often and too much. It is accepted for women to voice their fears openly about dangerous acts and it is permissible for a woman to cry, as long as it does not interfere with her functioning and provided that she does not become a "cry baby". There are accepted times for the male child to weep, such as crying about the death of a horse or the loss of a calf. In recalling such incidents, men did not deny their emotional involvement, although they did indicate embarrassment.

Ridicule is another means used to ensure conformity of behaviour as well as conformity of norms. Failure on the part of a child to perform a chore leads to derogatory statements regarding intelligence or maturity or, in the case of boys, their masculinity. For example, a father said to his nine-year-old son:

> ... do you mean to say you can't carry those buckets? (father picks them up and swings them as if to show they are very light) ... well, I guess you ought to stay in the kitchen if you can't carry them ...

Work and Responsibility: The View of Childhood

The dominant feature of the agricultural family – its fusion of familial and economic relationships – intrudes in an important way into the definition of parent-child relationships.

That all ranch and farm children are expected to help with chores is one of the explicit bases for the widespread belief that a farm or ranch is a good place to raise children. Growing up in the country, respondents insisted, contributes to the child's self-reliance and independence, while raising a child in the city or town does not offer the same possibilities. The work activities keep the child busy and "out of trouble". This is phrased:

> I've seen some kids from the city and they are useless ... They can't do a thing ... not even open and shut a gate. Living in the

country gives kids certain things over kids raised in the city. They learn responsibility and to be independent from things they do.

What is meant, in effect, is not that it is easier to raise a child in an agricultural setting, but that the characteristics which are valued – learning to work hard without complaining and to carry through an assigned task – can be taught in country settings more easily. The child is assigned chores he has watched others do and he learns to do them without complaining. He demonstrates self-reliance by learning the task without explicit instruction or without appealing for help from adults.

Although all children are expected to do chores, parental expectations for sons differ from those for daughters. Sons are potential successors and, as such, they are expected to work harder and show more interest in the enterprise. Sons have no options; daughters do. Daughters who prefer to remain at home and help their mothers are permitted to do so and, in fact, in those cases where their labour on the enterprise is not important, fathers suggest that they do so. The following quote illustrates these different expectations:

> J- (the ten-year-old daughter) doesn't like working outside, although sometimes she says it's better than some of the chores she has to do at home... but she never did go with her dad... and unlike her brother, she never did want to go.

> B- (the speaker's husband) is very good with M- (the eight-year-old son). He explains everything to him, takes him everywhere... M-'s gone with him since he was about four years old... to the irrigation plot, everywhere...

Obviously, the socialization into sex roles and their accompanying work expectations is complex. There is no one-to-one relationship between a parent's act and a child's response. The child is as complicated as the adult and certain behaviour on the adult's part will not elicit similar responses from all children. Thus, even if a father does take his daughter "everywhere" (as some fathers do) it would not mean that the daughter would necessarily enjoy agricultural work or prefer the "outside". However, the fathers who made special efforts to include their daughters in the enterprise activity, or those families where the mothers worked outside, do tend to raise daughters who are more interested and involved in agricultural production.

Where labour needs are great and there is little cash, boys and girls are regarded as important sources of labour. They begin to help at an earlier age and are able to put in a full day's work by the time they are thirteen or fourteen. The labour of children is preferred to that of a hired hand, since the children already "know what to do and you don't have to tell them the way you do a stranger".

The regional district history books are filled with stories of settlers who began work at ages thirteen and fourteen:

> My first job in Saskatchewan in 1909 (age thirteen) was taking a bunch of cattle from Jasper north to the Saskatchewan River ... Sometimes I would put in more time in the saddle than in bed ...

Children as young as eight years of age were called upon for work:

> In the spring of 1914 Dad and J- and son P- who was eight years old left for the homestead coming by freight ... they set up the (3) wagons, P- an eight-year-old ... his dad said, "P-, you are a big boy and must go along to help," and that he did ... (The drive was two days, the second day turned into a blizzard.) ... When they got to the top of the hill, they could see a small black house which was home, Dad said, "that's it son, head your horses to it ... "

Respondents made the point over and over again that in the past children did "real" jobs:

> Kids aren't treated the same today. They're not given major responsibility ... they're sheltered and expected to get an education ... be a gentleman or lady.

The frontier, of course, was full of young men "making it on their own". In a sense this pattern continued into the depression, when an adolescent was required to do an adult's work in order to make ends meet. The adults who had such experiences are today's parents and grandparents. They do not think it necessary that their children (grandchildren) experience such hardships, and many take the position that it is good that they don't have to. However, they do feel that young people should recognize their good fortune and not take it for granted. There is an implication that the young generation (post 1950) "spends too much", "goes too much", and "wants too much". Thus the older generation will criticize their children for not understanding the "meaning of a dollar", or the "meaning of work":

> Dad repeated his old lessons to us. One went something like this — save every penny, nickel and dime. Make a soft nest and drop them in. To your surprise they will hatch out a batch of money called dollars. There is a lot of truth to it ... but you can't tell it to the kids today.

At the same time, the parental generation is part of a culture which emphasizes consumption and recreational wants, and can benefit from it with increased retirement leisure, television, trips and the like. As a consequence, along with the concern with "spoiling a child" and "giving them everything", they take pleasure in the fact that their children and grandchildren need not suffer the hardships they knew. The ambivalence is phrased as follows:

> Today kids get everything they want. They (the kids) don't appreciate things. They don't understand what it is to work or wait for things.
>
> Our kids never had to suffer. They don't know what it was like. They take all they have for granted.

But in alternative situations, they might say:

> It's natural to want to give kids what you never had ... you don't want them to have it the way you did.

Or,

> My kids won't have to go through what I did and I'm glad.

These respondents are caught, as are most parents in changing times, between desiring the best for their children and not being certain as to what is the best.

Parents, Children, and Maturity

Fathers and Sons

Parent-child expectations and obligations change with the maturing of the child and the aging of the parent. As noted earlier, although the ideal is economic independence from one's family, the young man cannot hope to enter the agricultural occupation without aid (and with few exceptions this aid is from father to son or father-in-law to son-in-law). Breimeyer[10] writes:

> In making possession of financial capital a condition for entry, agriculture differs sharply from industry. It is difficult for a person to enter farming in a role higher than semiskilled laborer without contributing financial capital, but even the top executives in business and commerce often attain their positions irrespective of how many shares of company stock they hold. This difference reflects the combining of capital holding and labor in single hands in agriculture and their almost total separation in industry ... To farmers themselves ownership is viewed not so much as a source of (imputed) return to investment as of a means to gain employment. For a farmer to invest in land is almost a case of his buying his job opportunity.

[10] Breimeyer, *op. cit.*, p. 80.

In 1963-1964, a viable ranch cost anywhere from $150,000 to $600,000; a farm between $35,000 and $150,000. These prices had increased by 15 percent to 20 percent in the early 1970s. Few young men have been able to accumulate the necessary capital for purchase and all look to the retiring generation for financial aid.

While there are similarities between ranch and farm succession practices, the amount of capital necessary to farm is less. It is possible for a young man who desires to farm to do so by renting or purchasing one-half section of land. He works with his father, sharing labour and equipment. He can rent or buy the farm through crop shares, thereby eliminating the problem of a large capital outlay. The credit available through government loans, banks, or private sources can often provide a significant fraction of his capital entry costs if he is willing to start small.[11] Of course, a one-half section farm (320 acres) is inadequate to support the young family and he still requires the financial assistance of his parents. He can expand or eventually take over his father's land at a later date. He can also supplement his income through casual labour with road construction crews, irrigation projects, or on local farms or ranches.

A ranch operation requires more land and more capital expenditure. The process of succession to his father's enterprise is, for the ranch son, a long and arduous process of apprenticeship in which he earns "shares" for his work. The successor is, in effect, a hired hand who gradually acquires an investment in the enterprise. Ideally, by the time of his father's death, the ranch is in the hands of the son or the property is finally transferred by testament. However, the son must be willing to wait until that time and accept the controls placed upon him by his father. Where a father is aging – or in precarious health – and convinced of his son's ranching skills, he may be anxious for his son to assume operation of the enterprise and facilitate the take-over. In this case, the sale of the ranch will be at a price far below market value and the purchase agreement between father and son will be highly favourable to the son. However, where the father is young and in good health, and has not made preparation for his son's entrance into the occupation through intensifying his production or through adding land, the son must be willing to wait and be content with his hired hand position.

In families with more than one son, the decision-making aspect of succession is difficult and embarrassing, especially if all the boys entertain hopes of succession. Competition and conflict among them – and

---

[11] A new land policy program has been initiated (1972) by the Saskatchewan Provincial Government: the Saskatchewan Land Bank Commission buys acreage from farmers who desire to retire and then leases the land at a modest fee (5¾ or 5.75 percent of the property's value) to young would-be farmers. Applicants are restricted to those who have had incomes of less than $10,000 for a period of three years and whose net worth is not greater than $60,000.

among the sons and their father – can be severe. This situation has become the theme of many novels about ranching families and, for that matter, is similar to the European nobility and gentry in those cases where there are no set rules (such as primogeniture) to ease the conflicts.

In the past, multiple inheritance had been a solution. However, in the contemporary period, leased grazing land has been barred from subdivision by government law and the ranching enterprise depends decisively on the availability of this leased land. The land bureau must approve the successor and will not approve the breakup of lease land into units which they consider too small. This is not to say that multiple succession is impossible, but only that in most cases the enterprises would have to undergo expansion in order to make it possible.

As noted above, there are not established rules which simplify the transfer of property. Local residents view the choice of son for succession as subject to idiosyncratic factors and historical accidents. There is a slight tendency toward *de facto* ultimogeniture due largely to the fact that the father is often old and in failing health at the same time that his youngest son reaches maturity.

However, the age of the father at the time of the son's maturity is not the only factor involved in succession practices. Also important is the son's willingness to accept the father's authority. The data indicates that, in most cases, the decision as to which of several sons took over the ranch was based on which of the sons got along best with the father.

The willingness to accept a dependent status is a character trait usually associated with an individual who is cheerful, loyal, hardworking, and with the ability to defer gratification. Curiously, these traits are diametrically opposite to the idea of independence and individualism, also vigorously defended in Jasper. The son who pleases his father has learned that agriculture is hard work and that its rewards are sufficient to make it worthwhile, and he is willing to settle for a long period in a dependent role. Those unwilling to do so leave the community, and their departure helps to maintain the regional traditions of management and father-son relations.

The age and health of the father at the time his son reaches his majority becomes an important factor in the control exercised by the father and the subsequent dependence of the son. As the father ages, he becomes more dependent upon his son as a source of labour. Acceptable labour is difficult to get and, in one sense, the aging father is as dependent upon his son to continue the operation as the son is dependent upon the father to begin his own operation. Where the son desires to enter agriculture, this complementarity of needs works to the advantage of both father and son.

Ideally, by the time the son has reached his majority and is ready to take over the operation of the enterprise, his father is ready to retire. The son has been accumulating shares in the enterprise for his work which permits him to "buy" or rather refinance the enterprise from the father. Such coincidence of maturity and autonomy of action is not frequent. More commonly, the father is not ready to retire when the son reaches his majority and the latter must wait.

The waiting period is a difficult one for both father and son; their conflicts (regardless of good will and good intentions) permeate the family relationships. The mother acts as a buffer, placating the father and supporting her son. The culture values independence and autonomy; the move forward exercising the prerogative of adulthood by the young man involves the cutting of family ties, yet he is bound into a family-held enterprise and, in order to enter his desired occupation, he must remain under the authority of his father/boss. We have called this "bound-dependency".

It is during this period that young men often leave home and, using the skills they have learned on the enterprise, work in construction or as ranch hands. They take jobs which do not demand a long-term commitment, retaining their goal of entry into agriculture. This period varies between two and ten years. It permits both father and son to reconcile their differences and gives the young man time to try other things and make up his mind about taking over.

This "waiting period" is more commonly experienced by ranch than farm sons, since the ecomomic and ecological requirements for farming are more flexible than for ranching. The young man who works with his father sharing equipment and labour could rent or buy a farmstead through crop shares, eliminating the problem of a large capital outlay. Of course, he still requires the support of his family as he slowly accumulates sufficient resources for a viable enterprise.

Upon the son's return and statement of his desire to enter the occupation, the role the father assumes is crucial. The father who is able to "let go" and permit his son to innovate and take some genuine responsibility obviously facilitates the succession process.[12] This was recognized intuitively by a few fathers who divided the operation of the farm into cattle and grain production, giving their son complete control over one or the other.

The son who does not want to commit himself to take over the enterprise presents other problems. Where both parents have invested their energies in the establishment of the enterprise, and where they have only one son, succession is usually a much-desired eventuality. Continuity of family name is important, and succession of the son is viewed as one indication of success of the parents, particularly the father. The father, as operator, has been able to establish and develop an

---

[12] Murray A. Straus, "Societal Needs and Personal Characteristics in the Choice of Farm, Blue-Collar, and White-Collar Occupations by Farmers' Sons," *Rural Sociology*, 29(1964), 408-425.

"Finally, a new house!" The new farm house, postponed for twenty years, placed beside the old homestead house which remains potentially usable.

Brother and sister innoculating calves.

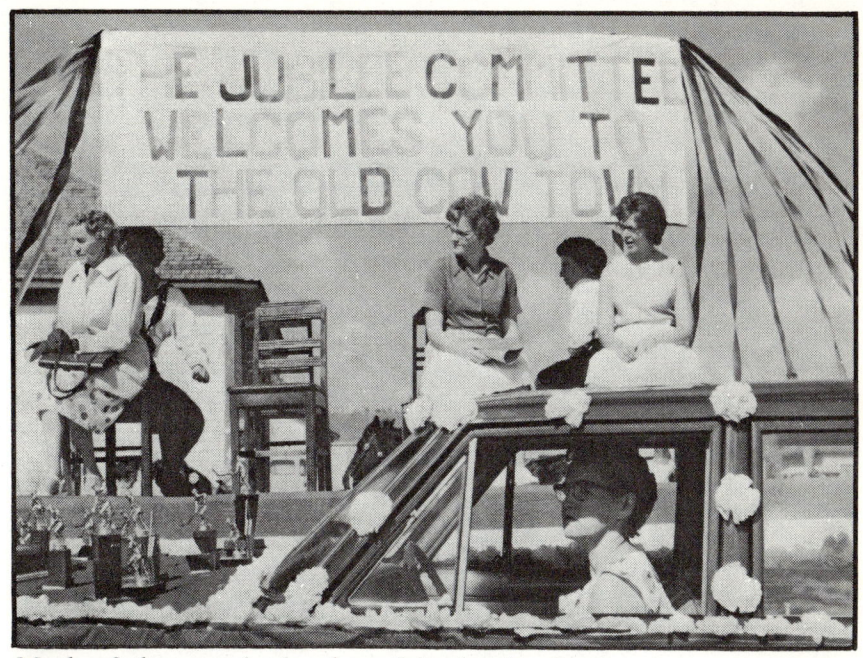

Much of the organizational participation by Jasper women reinforces community traditions. Here women, in the background, serve as judges for a Jubilee parade, while the woman on the right drives a float.

Men and Boys: the Western image.

enterprise which should be good enough to be wanted by the son. In the pragmatically minded farming community, as opposed to the typically more ideologically concerned ranching families, agriculture is seen as a good life, but only if the enterprise is "worth it":

> If your father has enough land so it pays to stay, and if you like it, then a fellow will stay ... or if they can get the money to buy their own place, they will stay and farm. But you can't expect anyone to stay on a two-bit place.

If the enterprise is poor, then it is better to do something else – assuming, of course, that there are alternatives. There are men in Jasper who tried different jobs and returned to farm on those "two-bit" places. One young farmer who had returned after six years as a bank clerk in Calgary told us:

> You know, it takes a certain type of person to make out in this country. You have to like this kind of life. We both like sports, both play on the ball teams. And we made out a little golf course out there in the field, and Mary and I go out there and play around. We like to fish too. We enjoy life like this, and it doesn't cost anything.

Where the son desires to try alternatives to agriculture, and where the enterprise can support two households, the son must reject the father's goals. If the son leaves, the father is disappointed, even though later he may be proud of his son's achievements.

However, although they are a minority, Jasper has some well-established operators who, with their wives, desire their sons to leave the farm or ranch for alternative occupations. These men do not tie succession of their sons to their personal concepts of success. Their view of agriculture is that it is just one way among others to make a living and that urban life holds greater opportunities for their sons. These men and women will be described more fully in Chapter VII.

Mothers and Daughters

As indicated earlier, the standardized expectations for the young girl virtually ensure her migration from the region if she is not able to marry within it. By high-school age, the rural girl is virtually indistinguishable from her urban counterpart. It is at this period that teenage girls encourage their mothers to "dress up", shorten (or lengthen) their skirts and fix their hair. These concerns also extend to decorating the house and consequently there are new pressures within the household for consumption expenditures. Mothers, responsible for the consumption style of the family household, are subject to new pressures – hard to resist – from their daughters. Mothers tend to yield to their daughter's demands, and mother and daughters often form a "female alliance" which competes with the enterprise for capital. This is rationalized in terms of the father/operator's expenditures on machinery compared with much smaller expenditures for clothing or furniture. However, the size of the purchase does not necessarily suffice as a rationale. "Smallness" also can be used to avoid expenditures on household items. As one woman noted:

> When I was first married my mother-in-law said to me that they (the men of the household) get a tractor or machinery or whatever they need. But if we need something then it's called "too small" and doesn't matter.

While the potential for the female alliance exists when daughters come of age, its realization is dependent upon the development phase of the enterprise. During the intensive development stage, all adult family members agree that alternative expenditures have low priority. Once beyond that stage, the operator's goals may vary: he may want to expand the enterprise or he may be content to maintain its current level. It is only when the enterprise has passed tnrough the intensive development stage that the "female alliance" can hope to influence decisions about allocation of capital. However, an appropriate position in the enterprise development cycle does not ensure, by itself, that the preferences of mother and daughter coincide. In cases where there are one or more sons, the mother may support her husband's policy of expansion of the enterprise, with its necessary contraction of domestic consumption. As phrased by one woman:

> When it comes to spending a dollar I always ask myself, "what is it going to make?" ... if you buy a rug, well you have a rug, but if you use the same money and buy a cow, the cow has calves and with the calves you can get the rug, but you still have the cow.

The deferment of consumption goods or "doing without" can be effectively rationalized by the woman and the rest of the household in terms of securing the son's future. After all, even if the son likes rugs, it is cows which are his future wealth. This rationale does not hold for the daughter since, with few exceptions,[13] she cannot accumulate any equity in the enterprise.

More commonly, the new consumption demands coming from the daughter complement the preferences of the mother, rather than conflict with them. In this case, the "female alliance" is forged. The de-

---

[13] Among some livestock-producing families, children of both sexes "earn" cows – a calf can be considered as payment for help within the household and on the enterprise. Their cows become a form of savings for future use which can be converted to cash when needed. In some cases, youngsters are given a choice of either cash wages or wages in the form of cows for their summer work.

bates and disputes of the following years will vary according to the commitment of the father or sons to the goal of expanding the enterprise. Where the father's focus is on continued development of the enterprise, and where this requires the reinvestment of all capital, conflicts arise. Mothers who have traditionally acted to minimize family consumption find it harder to restrain their daughters. They do not want to subject their daughters to the same kind of hardship they experienced. Yet at the same time, they recognize the importance of investment in the enterprise for their future security. Their role becomes that of mediating between enterprise and household. One solution is to initiate wages for the daughter's work on the enterprise, another is for the mother to defer her own personal gratification in deference to her daughter's. An alternative solution is to substitute personal labour for expenditure on consumption items: women and girls often make their clothes and engage in craft activities and house decoration. Some mothers feel unable to meet their daughter's desires. But no matter what form the response takes, the daughter's needs always stay one step ahead of an easy response to them. This has been observed among urban young people as well and probably reflects the fact that two processes are intertwined: the consumption demands are born of an awareness of the outside world and a groping toward defining one's position in it, but this awareness signifies another event, namely, that the young woman feels that she is being held on too short a rein and that she deserves more autonomy. The maternal response in this situation often is to adopt a stance of behavioural permissiveness. This permissiveness may be a conscious effort on the mother's part to compensate for her inability (or unwillingness) to satisfy her daughter's consumption desires. With respect to social activities, the permissive stance may signify a concession to, or a recognition of, the daughter's age and sense of growing maturity. It may result from the mother's dissatisfaction with her own lot or an idea that childhood is a unique experience, to be indulged. As one informant noted, "you are only young once and she will have to work hard enough soon enough." But no matter what the source, permissiveness of mother *vis-à-vis* daughter is criticized by both the older generation – mother and mother-in-law – and by the woman's peers in terms of "spoiling" and not teaching children how to "manage money". However, one should remember that what may be viewed by the outside as "permissiveness" may be viewed by the participants as minimal concessions which are necessary for maintaining family relationships on an even keel.

Obviously, given a limited income, not all wants can be gratified regardless of intentions and, since it is the mother's role to set consumption limits, this is a constant area for argumentation (as is the daughter's emerging sexuality). These issues are essentially unresolved until the daughter's marriage. The mother is part of the community which effectively establishes and reinforces the cultural prescriptions. Even though a mother may not agree with the norms, and even if she has been subject to gossip when she was young (for example, if she was pregnant before marriage), she does not want her daughter and family to be subject to the opprobrium which she knows will be forthcoming if her daughter does not follow the rules. Thus, the mother tends to grow more conservative as the interaction proceeds – more concerned with "what people will say". And, inevitably, the fear of "what people will say" becomes in itself a point of disagreement between mother and daughter, since neither of them share the same reference group nor the custodial view of the family. The daughter simply lacks the same prestige stake in the family's reputation.

Grandparents, Parents, and Grandchildren

As the parent ages, the parent-child relationship subtly changes from economic dependence of child on parent to social dependence of parent on child. Although the parent may still retain economic independence, his emotional investments in his offspring are such that with aging and the loss of collateral and ascending kin, he becomes more dependent upon the younger, particularly his offspring and family.

With few exceptions, children in Jasper have close ties with at least one set of grandparents. Where there has been father-son succession, retirement is primarily within the region – on the enterprise, in Jasper town, or in one of the villages. Where there has been no succession, the older generation entertains more alternatives for retirement places. Grandparents who live in the town where the country child attends school are important social aids to both child and parents. Since school children are dependent upon the school bus for transportation, unless they have alternative means of transportation or a place to stay in town, they cannot participate in pre- and post-school activities.

While the specific role behaviour of "indulgent" grandparent has been noted elsewhere,[14] in Jasper there is no formalized definition of this grandparental role. Rather, the grandparent offers situational support, as well as functioning as an active participant in the daily life of the agricultural family.

The grandparents' home has a distinct function – different from the homes of other kinsmen – since it is seen as a permissible alternative to the child's own household. Similarly, household help and child care by grandparents is viewed differently from that provided by siblings or other kinsmen. Women say that although their mother (mother-in-law) is an important help to them, they do not reciprocate in

---

[14] A. R. Radcliffe-Brown, "Introduction", in A. R. Radcliffe-Brown and D. Forde, eds., *African Systems of Kinship and Marriage* (London: Oxford University Press, 1950).

the usual sense, as they commonly do in their relationships with friends and peers. Rather they feel *obliged* to permit their mothers or mothers-in-law to help *them*. If they did not permit them to participate in child care or help with heavy chores (for example, cooking for a harvesting or branding party), the older woman would feel hurt or insulted. The continuation of the care of children and household activities has a function for the woman similar to the continuation of enterprise activities for the man. Their usefulness signifies and maintains a sense of well-being and identity.

With collaterals or with kinsmen other than parents, a count is kept as to the balance sheet of help, but with parents, the reciprocity is defined as permission for the older parents to continue to participate in their children's lives. This participation can be viewed by their adult children either as interference or aid, and the younger couple must balance the two. For most the balance is positive; for a few there are continual battles.

Siblings

In contrast with the importance of maintaining continual ties between parents and child, the maintenance of ties between siblings is highly variable, depending in later years upon the social situation and personal affect.[15] In childhood, siblings are valued as play-group companions and the only child, or the child who is born much later than his other siblings, is in a special situation where cousins or neighbours become more important as playmates.

The role of the older sibling is a special one: he teaches skills and supervises the behaviour of his younger siblings. The older sibling assumes many parental functions, particularly in situations outside of the enterprise. Older siblings, if living in the region and married, provide an opportunity for the younger siblings to manipulate parental demands and controls. They provide an alternative home and assurance to their parents of adequate supervision.

Siblings in the same general age grade are expected by parents to fight among themselves, but to present a solid front to those outside the household. Older children perform useful tasks much earlier than younger siblings and not surprisingly this becomes a source of argument between them. Where the oldest child is an able and competent worker, his position of eldest gives him authority (as well as physical dominance) over his younger siblings, which keeps the conflict in control. His authority permits him to deflect some of the chores and to move to more desirable tasks. There is a hierarchy of preferred jobs on the enterprise – tasks which involve machinery are preferred to others.

---

[15] D. Sweester presents similar findings. See *idem* "The Structure of Sibling Relationships," *American Journal of Sociology*, 76 (1970), 47-58.

The former are viewed as work, the latter as chores, and work is considered more manly and desirable. When the younger sibling outstrips his older brother, bitter conflict – sometimes continuing into adulthood – is often the result.

Where the oldest child is a girl and her labour is needed on the enterprise, she usually becomes proficient enough so that little brother can never quite "catch up". We have six cases in our notes where the father preferred the girl as a hand to the exclusion of her younger male siblings. One consequence was the development of rivalry and tension between the girls and the other family members over the father's approval and affection. A common dynamic is the increased closeness of mother and son with the consequent fear that the son is not "manly", but a "mama's boy", adding to the father's impatience with what he considers his son's ineptitude. Although not without extracting a psychological toll, this kind of family constellation is resolved with the marriage of the daughter and the maturation of the son. In some instances – we are aware of three – this situation has had continuing consequences for both the girl and her male sibling because the young man, who is the successor, has never felt as competent as his older sister.

With maturation, proximity is an important factor in the degree to which siblings maintain their close ties.[16] Male siblings are able to work together as long as their father continues as head of the enterprise. However, without the authority of an older head, few enterprises operated by brothers continue for more than a period of five to ten years. In one successful operation, one of the brothers was unmarried. It may be that his bachelor status allowed him to make fewer economic demands upon the enterprise. Being single may also have enabled him to contribute disproportionately to meeting the demands of the enterprise, since he had fewer obligations which might have diverted him from responding to enterprise needs. The unmarried brother commonly took his meals at his sister-in-law's table and in general was incorporated into his brother's household. This relationship apparently provided the positive elements of a trade-off which balanced his smaller economic return and greater contribution to the enterprise, if in fact these were the outcome of his partnership with his married brother. In a second case, one of the brothers was much older and his age gave him a position similar to that of a father.

The typical cycle of brother-brother enterprise operation is that upon the death of the father, where both had been working with the father prior to his death, both inherit equally and attempt to operate jointly. Commonly there is an attempt to divide the operation of the enterprise into specific areas of competence. However, there are inevitable conflicts with regard to priorities. These conflicts eventually lead to an

---

[16] See Elaine Cumming and David Schneider, "Sibling Solidarity: A Property of American Kinship," *American Anthropologist*, 63 (1961), 498-507.

agreement by one brother to sell.[17] Such agreements are commonly made at the point in the family cycle when the children of the brother who will remain are adolescent. The children take over the additional labour requirements, without the same expenditure of income, and it is possible to buy out the brother who is leaving. The sale makes possible a father-son operation with the hope of the son succeeding to the enterprise, reinforcing the instrumental importance of the father-son bond over the sibling bond.

The Wider Kin Group

In an earlier chapter the role of the extended kin as social control agents was discussed. The extended kin who live within the region also serve other functions. There are a wide range of adult figures with whom the rural Jasper child is familiar and who provide alternative developmental models as well as assistance on tasks. In contrast with many suburban children,[18] the Jasper child has an opportunity for social relationships with people in all stages of the life cycle. When the older generation retires, they retire nearby – either on the family enterprise or to a house in a local town – and remain an integral part of the daily round of life. In addition, there is little age segregation in social celebrations. Regardless of the event being celebrated, these occasions are usually family affairs. A child's birthday party is not only for the child and his friends, but is attended by the entire kin and quasi-kin group as well. The other adults provide experiences for the young child, such as frequent invitations to accompany them on a trip. They also serve to mediate between the young child and his parents since they are independent, although not uninvolved, observers.

The extended kin also perform useful socialization functions. Aunts, uncles, cousins, and other relatives make demands upon the child to "perform" to demonstrate his growth and cleverness. For example, delight is taken in "showing off" behaviour of the child which is considered smart. Verbal games are played in which the child just beginning to talk is asked such questions as "Who lives in this house?" or "Who lives in Auntie Sue's house?" Here the child is expected to list the names of the family members of each household and their kin titles. Other typical questions are "Who drives a Ford car?", "Who drives a Mercury car?", "How do you cross a street?" and "What does Uncle Andy do?"

[17] Hammel reports a similar process in the formation and fission of the Serbian zadruga where brothers whose own sons are approaching maturity tend to hive off. See E. A. Hammel, "The zadruga as process," in Peter Laslett, ed., *Household and family in past time* (Cambridge: Cambridge University Press, 1972), pp. 335-374, especially p. 371.

[18] See P. E. Slater, *The Pursuit of Loneliness* (Boston: Beaver Press, 1971), p. 9; U. Bronfenbrenner, *Two Worlds of Childhood: U.S. and U.S.S.R.* (New York: Russell Sage, 1970); and J. R. Seeley, R. A. Sim, and E. W. Loosley, *Crestwood Heights* (New York: John Wiley and Sons, 1956).

Similar word games are played which show that the child knows the correct title and address of the family members or where each family member works. These games are not restricted to teaching the child his family relationships, but also include teaching numbers, the meaning of signs, safety rules, and health practices. This level of interest and concern in the growth and maturation of their young kinsmen is maintained throughout their lifetime.

Although emphasis has been placed upon the interest and concern shown the younger generation by the older, this is not to say that there is no reciprocity. The younger person reciprocates the interest shown him through the continued inclusion of the senior generation in his social world. Children visit with grandparents, aunts, and uncles regularly. They run errands, shovel snow, and manage a myriad of chores. While some visiting is *pro forma* and some tasks are regarded as "chores", as obligations to be fulfilled, much of the social interaction between senior and junior generations is regarded as more than obligatory.

The aspects of extended kinship described in this chapter are somewhat idealized but, in general, the pattern is consistent in Jasper families. Bronfenbrenner and Slater,[19] two writers concerned with problems of contemporary suburban life (particularly those concerning the socialization of children), have commented on the narrowness and paucity of social experiences of the suburban child.[20] However, it is important to remember that the richer interaction available to children in Jasper involves costs as well as rewards. There is, also, a general narrowness of social experience in rural life. Young people phrase it in terms of "nothing to do" and "dullness". There are many routines; life is predictable. Parents verbalize it as "safety" for their children, what makes Jasper a "good place", an "easy" place to bring up children.

At the same time that these predictable social interactions are seen as aids to child rearing, the isolation from new experiences and from peers is also seen as a disadvantage. This is particularly true of a younger generation of parents who are attuned to contemporary child-rearing literature which emphasizes the importance of age-graded play groups. Such parents encourage their children's participation; however, that type of participation does not necessarily make new inputs either conceptually or socially, since the participants of the social group are already members of the network. It is here that members of an extended kin group living outside the region can become important agents in expanding opportunities and in presenting a world view.[21]

[19] *Ibid.*
[20] Also see Seeley, Sim, and Loosley, *op.cit.*
[21] See S. Kohl and J. W. Bennett, "Succession to Family Enterprises and the Migration of Young People in a Canadian Agricultural Community," in K. Ishwaran, ed., *The Canadian Family* (Toronto: Holt, Rinehart and Winston of Canada, Ltd., 1971), pp. 203-224.

CHAPTER VII

Women & the Family Enterprise

The preceding chapters have explored the expectations for role behaviour within the Jasper family and for social roles in age and sex categories. This chapter will focus on the participation of women in the family enterprise and the variations in women's roles, which we portray as a series of type cases, of what we call "family orientations". Not all women will "fit" the particular types precisely, but they include all relevant variants of the participation styles of most women in Jasper country families. The following table shows the distribution of the types of family orientations in our sample of the agricultural population:

TABLE 11: Distribution of Family Households with Defined Orientations, 1962-1972

	1962		1972	
	No.	%	No.	%
Families with Enterprise Development as a Major Focus (The Berry Family)	27	30	22	29
Families Who Consider Alternatives to Agriculture (The Slenko Family)	22	25	21	27
Families Committed to the Continuity of Kinship Control of the Ranch (The Hillman Family)	18	20	17	22
Families Willing to Defer Consumption in Exchange for Benefits of Rural Life (The Landsdorf Family)	15	17	14	18
Families Who Want to Leave Agriculture	7	8	3	4
TOTALS	89	100	77	100

Common to all typologies are problems involved in the choice of factors used for categorization and the assumption that these do not vary independently but are linked in some manner. The factors used to characterize family households are based upon both native and observer categories. They are: (a) the role of the woman in the enterprise; (b) parental expectations and aspirations for children; (c) conjugal expectations associated with the role of spouse; (d) social participation of adult members among kin and community; and (e) ideological justifications for these various expectations and aspirations.

In examining the variation in the woman's activity within the enterprise, it is important to remember that household and enterprise are composed of the same individuals but have differing goals. Household and enterprise are mutually dependent. These two entities can be viewed as sets of competing claims upon the members, forming a conflict which must be continually resolved. Each family develops its own patterns of resolution. The woman, in her role of housekeeper and quartermaster, is crucial in setting the styles of consumption and in establishing the level of living that is considered "acceptable". Similarly, in her role of mother, she is responsible for the socialization of her children. Her hopes for herself, for her children's role in the family enterprise and, eventually, in the larger world of school and regional organization will have consequences for the family's social and economic prospects in Jasper.

To achieve both enterprise development and a rewarding family life, the family members must share a strong commitment to work with one another and to do so for long hours. Family members must accede to delayed consumption wants, since where family members are unwilling to forego consumption, the economic stability of the enterprise is threatened. Thus, although it may be the father who, as head of the enterprise, initiates development, his success or failure is dependent upon the consent of the family.

The technological constraints of the enterprise also affect definitions of "need" for household labour. Where the enterprise can substitute machine labour for human labour – as in straight grain farm operations – "needs" for household participation in enterprise activities are less and family members have fewer demands on their time; they are free to organize their time according to their own interests. Where the technological demands of the enterprise are labour-dependent – as in cattle ranching – the organization of the household's time and labour will be more relevant to the success of the enterprise.

The developmental phase of the enterprise also affects household participation. In the early period of enterprise development – the period of establishment – all farm and ranch families must defer consumption and centre their activity upon the enterprise. Deferment of gratification during this period is taken for granted as part of the "starting out" process. Typically such a family household is young, and both husband and wife see their future as one of working together for the same relatively modest goals: some security of income and a "decent" place to live and raise children. However, where deferment of gratification continues longer than anticipated, different constellations of family household behaviour emerge as consequences of the role taken by the wife, a topic discussed later in this chapter. Let us begin with the participation of the woman in the enterprise.

Women's Participation in the Enterprise

Women contribute to the enterprise in the following ways: (1) deferring both personal and household consumption; (2) serving as bookkeepers, accountants, and resources for information regarding public agencies and bureaucratic regulations which affect the enterprise; (3) performing physical labour; (4) providing social relational skills and network links to other enterprises; (5) in a few cases, providing cash income through full- or part-time jobs. Finally, in a very small number of cases, women – without the help of a spouse – operate the enterprise. (Table 12 indicates the distribution in the sample.)

TABLE 12: Women's Contribution to Enterprise Production, 1962-1972

	1962								1972							
	Grain Farm		Mixed Farm		Livestock		Total		Grain Farm		Mixed Farm		Livestock		Total	
	No.	%	No.	%	No.	%	No.	%	No.	%	No.	%	No.	%	No.	%
Deferment*	1	11	12	25	4	14	17	20	1	14	10	33	2	7	13	20
Bookkeeping	–	–	14	29	4	14	18	21	1	14	7	23	4	15	12	19
Labour	1	11	1	2	5	18	7	8	–	–	1	3	3	11	4	6
Social Relation Skills	–	–	2	4	5	18	7	8	–	–	–	–	5	18	5	8
All of the above	2	22	17	38	4	14	23	27	2	28	9	30	5	18	16	25
Cash Income	3	33	1	2	2	7	6	7	2	28	1	3	1	4	4	6
No Contribution	1	11	–	–	1	4	2	2	1	14	1	3	3	11	5	8
Operating Head	–	–	–	–	3	11	3	3	–	–	–	–	4	15	4	6
Impede Enterprise Activity	1	11	1	2	–	–	2	2	–	–	1	3	–	–	1	2
TOTAL	9		48		28		85		7		30		27		64	

*Where women contribute both willingness to defer and another skill, for example, bookkeeping, they have been counted for that skill.

Some women contribute in all of these ways; some in only one or two; in a few cases there is no contribution (as long as one ignores the cost of household labour); and in even fewer, women are actual impediments – that is, their household behaviour and the behaviour they encourage in their children are detrimental to the enterprise. We will discuss these in turn.

The Wife as Active Participant in the Family Enterprise

The largest group of women are active contributors to the enterprise in all or nearly all ways: they share their husbands' goals and are willing to delay the accumulation of housekeeping aids. They share with their spouses expectations of children's participation in the work of the enterprise, and thus reinforce the husband's position as manager/head.

Social experiences of the children are approved and encouraged where a positive relationship is perceived between those activities and enterprise goals. For example, parents prefer to encourage their children's participation in 4-H clubs – where there is a potential carry-over for enterprise productivity – rather than participation in a club which is devoted to the development of horseback riding skills. Within these families there is an important explicit ideological position that working together is "good". Others in the community, seeing how well the family members work together, consider these families "close". We call them "Enterprise Focused Families".

"Eleanor Berry" is typical. She married Walter Berry in 1937; she was a teacher in Jasper school, he the eldest son of a homestead farmer who had settled north of Jasper in 1908. As was common among the children of the settling generation, Walter had little formal schooling (73 percent of the operators over the age of fifty in 1964 had less than eighth-grade education).

Upon their marriage, they moved to the Berry family homestead which Walter purchased from his father for a nominal sum. Mrs. Berry continued to teach for a year after they were married, until she became pregnant. They rented adjacent land on crop shares, finally buying 1440 acres in 1948. At this time they slowly began to build up a herd of cattle. A second child, a daughter Linda, was born subsequently.

In 1956 Berry's son, Jim, was sixteen years old and interested in farming, particularly in developing cattle production. He left school in tenth grade and worked full-time with his father. (Sons of families with this orientation not uncommonly leave school prior to their completion of grade 12. This was more common in the period 1955-1962 than 1964-1972 as indicated in Table 13.)

During this period, Berry senior added more land. The addition of the last parcel of land in 1963 of ten quarters (1600 acres) meant that the enterprise was big enough to concentrate on cattle, and big enough to support two households.

Although Linda Berry helped with the agricultural work, her potential as a full-time hired hand was never fully utilized by her father/boss, and she was never considered as a potential successor. Her early marriage (1963) to a neighbouring ranch son expanded the Berry's labour exchange network: she and her husband joined with the Berry family for harvest and branding activities, her brother reciprocating in kind.

In 1964, in anticipation of Jim's marriage, a formal succession agreement was signed and the senior Berrys moved to the town of Jasper, leaving the farmhouse for the young couple. The farmhouse in which the senior Berrys had lived was large, well maintained, comfortable, and old. Although the kitchen had all the conveniences – water, propane stove, freezer, and refrigerator – there were few of the niceties of the modern kitchen, particularly cabinets and counter space. In 1967 remodelling of the kitchen was high on the young couple's list of priorities. Mrs. Berry's comments about the changes that the young couple wanted to make in the kitchen leave little doubt of the ambivalence she held about her daughter-in-law's set of values:

> I don't know ... I lived for twenty years without electricity, and it was hard, but we did fine ... If they want to go into debt for a kitchen it's their business ... we went into debt for land. But times have changed and credit is easier now.

The move to town was not without difficulty for the senior Berry couple. As Mrs. Berry said:

> It's not easy to give up everything you worked so hard for. In the beginning I was always running out to the farm every day. You want to keep going back to see if the things you planted are being taken care of ... if your chickens are doing well ... Life in town is much easier ... our house is new and we have a nice garden here ... We are thinking of taking a trip next year too ... It's better for Walter being in town ... his back was getting bad ... but we still miss the farm.

Mrs. Berry shared with her husband a strong commitment to enterprise development which was transmitted to the children of the household. There was also a fortuitous meeting of the needs for enterprise development and the availability of the son's labour – that is, as Berry added land, his son matured and was available (as well as competent) to assume greater participation in the enterprise activity.[1] Even more important, there was a fortunate congruence in the desire of the father to retire and the desire of the son to take over the enterprise.

The Ambivalent Farm Housewife

In contrast with the Berry family are the "Slenkos". They are representative of those Jasper families who consistently present alternative occupations to their children. Mrs. Slenko's contribution to the family

---

[1] See Figure 7.1, "Family Cycle and Enterprise Cycle" in J. W. Bennett, *Northern Plainsmen: Adaptive Strategy and Agrarian Life* (Chicago: Aldine Publishing Co., 1969), p. 229.

enterprise is in her willingness to defer consumption, but her goals – unlike Mrs. Berry's – point outside the enterprise and outside the region.

"Betty Slenko" was always ambivalent about rural life. She grew up on a marginal farm near the Slenko farm during the 1930s and married Howard Slenko, a second son of Ukrainian immigrants, in 1944. He was working for one of the large local ranchers, and she went to cook for them. At the time of their marriage Howard bought a half-section of land to which they moved in 1946.

Her family sold out and returned to the United States. At that time Mrs. Slenko thought she and Howard should do the same but, as she put it, he had "the ranching bug". He had worked for the large ranchers in the area as a hand from the time he was about fifteen years old. During this period he learned about cattle and decided that it was more profitable, as well as more to his liking, than straight grain farming. Through the years, they added cattle which they pastured on Howard's father's lease land. His father also helped by sharing machinery and by signing the note when the young Slenkos borrowed money.

Nevertheless, by 1950 there was constant talk in the family household of leaving the farm. By this time the Slenkos had two children and Mrs. Slenko suffered from chronic back trouble so that there was little she could do on the enterprise. In addition, Howard – a second son – had two brothers living in Medicine Hat who were "doing well" and, although Howard had worked closely with his father, his father's brother and his older brother, it was understood that his older brother would take over the parental place.

During this period (1950-1960) when the children were growing up, alternatives to the farm (which was, in the parlance of the region, a "two-bit place") were actively presented by the parents. Howard Slenko regretted his own lack of education and encouraged his son, a good student, to consider agricultural college. Each summer the Slenkos were able to visit with Mrs. Slenko's family in Montana, camping at various national parks, because Howard Slenko, unlike other diversified farmers, could rely upon his father and brother to take care of his stock.[2]

The Slenkos followed a course representative of those families who act to expand their world and the world of their children beyond the enterprise. Education is actively promoted as a means for success and most of these sons complete grade 12 (see Table 13). The farm is viewed as an alternative for the child who does not do well in school, who is not "smart":

---

[2] In Jasper, substantial improvement of the economic resources of the enterprise is almost always made through entering into livestock, particularly beef cattle, production. Adoption of cattle requires that considerable capital must be invested for breeding and pasturage. Furthermore, because cattle production also requires year-round labour, the customary long winter farm vacation has to be relinquished.

> My two older boys are smart in school and I'd like to send them to a university so they could be doctors or somebody who would give to society ... My younger boy is not so smart; if he wants to, he can be a farmer. It's the boys who are not good enough to do anything else who become farmers. Farming is the easy way out, not physically, but mentally. It's a hard life of work, but it doesn't take too much brains.

The Slenko children, and others like them, look outside the community to other occupations, and seek out activities locally which suggest such orientations; there is parental encouragement for their participation in extra-curricular school activities. Among these families, although the children work on the enterprise, priority is given to alternatives. Where this occurs, the role of the father as operator/head is diminished. Thus one father good-naturedly complained:

> I'm losing my hay crew ... but W- (wife) insists that the kids go to 4-H camp ... the kids don't know how to work anymore ... they're too busy to work ...

The emphasis outside the enterprise contrasts with the emphasis of the Berry family, where the primary focus is working together as a unit to build an enterprise which will be taken over by the son. In the latter case, schooling for the son and the energy and time it requires is a necessity, but extra-curricular activities, which often make schooling bearable, are viewed as a diversion from the family goal. Parents such as the Berrys, in judging their success as parents, emphasize the competence of the son as an agriculturalist rather than as a scholar. As Mrs. Berry said:

> ... Yes, we would have liked him to finish school, but he wanted to work with his dad and only thought about the farm, and he's doing just fine.

The lack of schooling only becomes a problem for the young man if he does not succeed his father. In fact, with few exceptions, the sons of these families remain within the region and follow agricultural occupations.

The Slenko enterprise and its related demands upon the family changed radically in 1962. Howard's older brother decided to leave the region and the patrimony of the senior Slenko enterprise became available to Howard. Ironically, at precisely the time that the eldest Slenko son left to go to agricultural college, Howard Slenko was left as a single operator in a situation where there had been four men working full time. The obvious solution to his need for labour was his older son and, in fact, after the first year of college Donald did return to work with his father for six months, but left to continue school, later going into a feed business in Calgary. His refusal to stay on the farm created great tensions within the family. Howard Slenko, although he needed his son's labour, could understand that Donald wanted to continue his schooling but, at the same time, he was offering his son exactly what *he* had wanted when *he* was twenty years old. Mrs. Slenko played the role of mediator between father and son, saying:

> Howard really needs Don now. He can't keep up with all the work. But Don wants to look around first before settling down and you can't blame him.

Although Slenko's daughter had helped with the agricultural work, her participation had been limited. In part, her limited experience was due to her own interests and desires, which were not primarily concerned with the farm; in part, it was due to the need for her to help her mother. Whatever the reason, her labour was never utilized by her father – a common situation even where the daughter is actively interested in the enterprise. In 1970, upon reviewing the failure of his older son to continue to work with him and still not secure about his younger son, Slenko indicated some regret that he had not more fully appreciated his daughter's potential, and perhaps her potential as a successor. He noted in this context:

> After spending four years in school in the Hat she went and married J- (a local mixed farmer) and now is doing all kinds of things she never did at home ... but the difference is, I guess, it's *her* place.

During this period (1965-1968), a hired hand had been employed. Slenko had managed to survive the past five years through a "holding" style of operation – he did little resource development but managed to maintain the traditional pattern of ranching established by his father and uncle. By 1970, when the younger son had graduated from twelfth grade and the older boy was well established in business in Calgary, both parents were placing great expectations on the younger boy to work with his father and eventually take over the enterprise. With the availability of his younger son as a full-time coworker, he was prepared to consider developing the enterprise by adding cattle and reseeding native pasture. The son, however, was not yet able to make the necessary commitment. Like his older brother, he was planning to go to agricultural college for the two-year course; he also wanted to travel. He thought he wanted to ranch with his father but wanted a few years before "settling down". He knew that his father needed him, but he talked about "his own life".

Parents such as the Slenkos encourage their sons (and daughters) to learn skills useful for participation in urban settings. Where these families do well financially, they allocate their discretionary income to family vacations, schooling, a cabin in the Cypress Hills; or, where the enterprise is isolated, they establish a town house. In this use of discretionary income they contrast with families like the Hillmans and Landsdorfs, found on both ranch and farm, who have an explicit ideological commitment to rural life as the "best life".

The Participating Ranch Wife

There is wide variation in the kind of participation of ranch women in enterprise activities, and many ranch wives follow patterns similar to their farm counterparts. However, the different productive technologies do cause two important general differences between ranch and farm women and their families. The greater spatial isolation of the ranch house from local centres of organizational activity inevitably means that ranch women in general are less involved in community social organizations.[3] Secondly, the ranch wife, in contrast with the farm wife, has the opportunity to extract from the enterprise recreational opportunities which include riding, horsebreeding, and racing. The women who develop these interests form a special group who emphasize their commitment to ranching, elaborating the western traditions and motif in their style of dress, their home furnishings, and their leisure activities.

The ranch wife who adopts ranching as an ideology (with all the trappings of Western life) takes an intense interest in the enterprise. These are women who emphasize the ranch family traditions and who talk about ranching as "a way of life":

> With us, ranching is more than a living ... it is a way of life, and we love it, we don't make much money, but there's other things in life ...

This type of woman enjoys the outdoors and completely accepts working with her husband. In this choice, she resembles the farm women who are active participants in enterprise activities. However, she is distinguished by her emphasis upon the *hobby* aspect which is special for ranching – an emphasis which in itself is an important consumption factor.

Although there is investment in nonutilitarian pursuits, there is also a long period of delayed gratification, particularly in household consumption. What is important to remember is that in these cases, the women are willing to defer consumption for long periods of time. The situation of "Mrs. Hillman" is illustrative of this situation.

"Mary Hillman", the daughter of a homestead farmer, married the third-generation rancher Roy Hillman in the late 1940s. They lived for a short period of time with the senior Hillmans, moving after the birth of their first child to a small cabin on the ranch. Roy, an only son, with no competitors for succession, worked for his father for wages and to accumulate equity in the ranch.

The period 1950-1960 was one of delayed gratification with few household amenities. The house was quite small (four rooms), but it did

---

[3] In 1962, 31 percent of ranch women did not participate in voluntary organizations; in 1972, this had increased to 36 percent (see Chapter IV).

have running water and electricity. In spite of the poor living arrangements, both Roy and Mary were able to invest in Arabian horse-breeding, taking the animals to shows throughout the province. Neither Roy nor Mary took part in any of the local church or fraternal organizations, although both were active in the local riding club.

In 1963, the senior Hillman retired from active operation of the ranch and Roy took over. The family now included four children between the ages of five and fifteen years. The older children were actively involved in the riding club and their pictures and trophies were displayed prominently in the living room.

When the senior Hillman died the following year, his wife moved to Jasper town and the younger family moved into the old ranch house. Both Roy and Mary had a number of ideas about the development of the ranch, and part of this development was to increase their Arabian stock. Mary's interest, as Roy's, centred on the enterprise – household consumption could wait. As she said:

> It sure is good to spread out. We were six people in four rooms too long. This is a good old house and all I really want to do is fix up the kitchen and bathroom. I don't expect to do much else, besides there are too many other things to do on the ranch ... after all, you can't milk a house.[4]

Five years later (in 1972) the Hillmans had completed many of their enterprise development plans. The oldest daughter was in college, and the oldest son, at age eighteen, refused to continue in school after completion of grade 11. This is a common pattern in educational careers for the children of these ranching families (see Table 13). Both Mary and Roy indicated that they would have liked him to continue with his schooling, but he had made it clear that he wanted to ranch and was working with his father. Although there was no explicit commitment, there seemed little doubt as to his probable succession.

For the ranch son today, as well as for his parents (in particular his father), ranching remains the preferred occupational goal as in the past. The generation of ranchers in control of enterprises in the nineteen-sixties and seventies had, with few exceptions, never seriously considered an alternative. Since it is believed important to maintain the continuity of the ranch within the family, even where a son might prefer doing something else, it is expected that he will take over the ranch after his father's death. This is particularly true where the ranch is well established. That the son will carry on the traditions of the family is for the most part made very clear and is accepted by the child. A Hillman son (the fourth generation) at the age of seven remarked:

> I'd like to go to the University and be a geologist and study rocks,

---

[4] The last sentence is a favourite aphorism among ranchers.

but probably Dad will be dead by then and I'll have to take over the ranch.

There are, however, indications of change in the expectations for the son's succession. Interviews with the younger ranch wives turned up statements emphasizing more freedom of choice:

> ... Well, we won't push our son into anything ... he can make up his own mind about what he wants to do.

However, the investment of self in the enterprise on the part of the parents makes it doubtful that their children (sons) will find themselves in a much different position than their fathers.

This, combined with the emphasis on ranching life as the good life and the financial and social security such ranch sons can hope to assume, makes few alternatives seem attractive despite the inherent conflict between father and son discussed earlier and despite the desire on the part of the mother to give her son a "free choice".

TABLE 13: Educational Level of Children from Households where Family Orientations have been Defined[1]

	1962				1972			
	Completed Less Than Grade 12		Completed Grade 12		Completed Less Than Grade 12		Completed Grade 12	
	Sons	Daughters	Sons	Daughters	Sons	Daughters	Sons	Daughters
Families with Enterprises Development Orientation	10	4	4	6	4	1	8	10
Families Who Consider Alternatives	2	3	12	6	2	–	15	13
Families Committed to Kin Continuity	12	1	4	6	5	–	3	6
Families Willing to Defer Consumption in Exchange for Benefits of Rural Life	4	6	3	7	1	1	3	1
Families Who Want to Leave Agriculture	–	–	4	3	–	–	–	2

[1]The figures for 1962 are based upon those children who left school between the years 1955 and 1963. The figures for 1972 are based upon those children who left school between 1964 and 1972.

The analogue to the ideologically committed ranch wife is the farm wife who, although she does not have the same sources for recreational pursuits, the interests in the enterprise, or the same economic resources as the ranch woman, nevertheless believes rural living the "best" or "only" way to live.

The Contented Non-Participant

"Helen Landsdorf", a city girl, met Jim while he was working in Calgary. Jim was the first son of four brothers. His father, originally from Norway, had first homesteaded in the southern part of the region in 1914. Jim finished eleventh grade and, after two years of working for his father, left the region and worked for the CPR for a period of eight years before deciding to return to the farm because of a growing distaste for wage work. By this time all of his siblings had left home; none were interested in farming.

When he returned to the farm in 1959, Jim rented two quarters of land, one from his father's brother (his uncle), the other from his father's brother's son (his cousin). He lived with his parents and helped his father who owned six quarters of land. The following year he married Helen. At that time, his parents moved to the town of Embassy leaving the original farmhouse for the young couple. Both Jim and his wife felt pinched economically. The house was old and dilapidated; there was no running water; the supply of ground water was inadequate, and water had to be hauled for the pigs and the garden. Decisions to drill a new well and to build a new house were postponed since all money was being invested in cattle. By 1964 Jim had thirty-five head which he pastured on the Community Pasture.

Helen Landsdorf had looked forward to the farm as an opportunity to "build" something. Furthermore it "was what Jim wanted to do", and she was prepared to help him. Her role in establishing the enterprise was primarily that of being willing to defer consumption. As she said:

> I don't do anything outside ... oh, I'll put in a garden — Jim does the plowing for me — but I won't haul water for it. If it dries out it just dries out ... I have enough to do at home.

The years between 1964 and 1968 (at which time Jim made his first land purchase) were spent working for his father, his father's brother, and his cousin. He added to his income by driving a school bus. When his uncle decided to retire in 1968, Jim was able to buy the two quarters on very favourable terms.

In 1970, at age forty-one, Jim Landsdorf still owned only two quarters of land; he rented two more quarters from his cousin. However, to establish a viable enterprise, he needed a minimum of an additional two quarters. He made up this deficit in resources by working for wages on his father's six quarters and by working as a labourer for the Irrigation District. Although he had managed to increase his cattle herd to eighty cows, a substantial amount, this was still only about one half the number required to make a living as a straight cattle operation. He expected to inherit his father's place "some day". His six-year-old son will be presented with the possibility of stepping into an economically viable operation slowly pieced together over the years by his father.

The Landsdorfs fixed up the old house in 1967 and, although heavily in debt in 1970 and acknowledging that they would never be rich, nonetheless they felt that they were living a fairly "good" life and Jim was "doing what he wanted".

In a marginal enterprise like the Landsdorfs', which operates at a subsistence level, additional income must come from other sources. Half of the small number of women who had jobs off the farm came from enterprises of this type (see Table 12). The more common solution is, as in the case of Jim Landsdorf, for the operator, rather than his wife, to take a second job. In these cases a far different constellation of family household behaviour emerges distinct from those families where women are actively involved in the enterprise.

Such men have two occupations: their own farm work and a full-time job; that is, they are *not* "part-time farmers". There is not much time for husband-wife companionship or for the man's assumption of "parenting" tasks. Furthermore, when the man works for another farmer or rancher, he is incorporated into the work exchange needs of his employer. Since he works with the operator, he joins his employer for meals, thus participating in the social life of the employer's family. He often does not join his own family for the large noon dinner and this means that the woman's responsibilities for the day-to-day operation of the household are less – if she desires them to be so. She is freed from the tasks required by cooking the noon dinner and can set her own work schedule. She is able to participate to the fullest in the social activities of women, extracting companionship and a sense of purpose, but accentuating the segregation of her social life from that of her husband.

However, it is necessary for her to accommodate to a restricted diet of consumption "niceties".[5] Both she and her husband acknowl-

---

[5] There is an interesting anomaly here when this kind of behaviour is contrasted with that of the urban woman who finds herself in similar economic straits. The urban woman typically enters the job market and removes herself from organization participation. In Jasper, however, there is active participation in women's clubs, behaviour which in urban settings is associated with the middle-income class; women who are "poor" from the urban standpoint can enjoy urban middle-income social amenities.

edge their difficult financial situation and the fact that they have not been able really to develop the "place", but neither accepts the alternatives which are available: working in a city or town in a semi- or unskilled jobs. Urban living, even though it may permit a higher income, is not acceptable to them. The rejection of urban living becomes an explicit ideological commitment. The term that is used is "we get by", and that they do.

Although these families avow their commitment to rural life, they are not isolated from urban life-styles. In particular, the changes in the lives of women during the decade of study should be noted. These changes not only involved important amenities of electricity and water but also included changes in appearance so that by 1971-1972, women were virtually indistinguishable in dress from their urban counterparts.

The changes in women's lives during the decade also are represented in the common symptoms of stress as seen in mental health statistics. In an earlier chapter we mentioned the decline in referral rates of women for psychiatric treatment during the period of study. It was suggested that the decline was in part associated with the relative increase in economic prosperity. Particular note should be taken of the dramatic change in the lives of women during the decade of research – a relatively short time. Increasing development of facilities in the region generally, and the increasing prosperity due to good farm prices and credit availability, made possible the purchase of labour-saving devices and many consumer items. It has also made better transportation possible, enabling greater mobility for women, and thus assuaging the effects of isolation – a problem for women commonly encountered in the psychiatric protocols.

The Woman Who Wants Out

These women are few in number. They include the women we consider to impede the work of the enterprise as well as a few (two in 1962; two in 1972) who have no effect upon the enterprise activity.

Where the enterprise is weak, and where there has been continued deferment of consumption and/or no definite end to hard work with few pay-offs, it is the woman who most commonly becomes disillusioned and presses for an alternative style of living.

One obvious solution is to sell out to a larger enterprise and leave agriculture, or go to work as a hired hand. However, although in effect the operator may be actually working full-time as a hired hand, so long as he retains his own enterprise, he retains the hope of establishing his "own place". He also retains his concept of self as a rancher or farmer, as distinct from a hired labourer. Although life may be easier for the wife of an urban factory worker, the husband is usually not prepared to consider such a change – the social costs of the change are too great.

The woman, however, encourages her children to leave agriculture; she feels that her daughters should not marry farmers and that her sons should do other things which will provide a better life. She phrases this in terms of "wanting something more" for her children. Where her husband agrees with her definition of "more" for the children, although still retaining his own view that urban life is not for him, he joins with his wife and encourages his sons to leave. In this case, they share a goal that centres on the success of their children who are encouraged to leave the farm.

This goal is one in which the pattern of activities is outside the enterprise. Since the enterprise is not the focus of family life, the sons and daughters are able to remain in town for school and social activities, and their mother encourages them to do so even at the economic expense of the enterprise (Jasperites refer to this as "milking the ranch (farm)."). In this practice they differ from the families who consider alternatives since the latter retain agriculture as a potential option for their sons; these families reject it. Urban kinsmen are important aids for schooling and for access to jobs. Mother and children leave the enterprise for extended periods of time during summer, reinforcing the lack of focus on the enterprise.

Where the husband does not agree with his wife that the struggle to farm is "not worth it", and where the wife's efforts for a better life for her children are personalized and focused against her husband's efforts to farm, there is inevitable derogation of the husband and continual conflict. The inference is that the children must choose between mother and father and their respective goals. Where there are only daughters and no sons, there is less conflict between father and children, since the expectations of the family are not bound up in the daughter's assumption of the agricultural operator role. Fathers in this situation can support their wives' efforts for the girls to "make something of themselves" without derogating their own occupational role.

The Woman as Enterprise Operator

These women are few in number (three in 1962; four in 1972). In all instances the enterprises are livestock operations. They comprise two types: the first is the woman who has taken over the operation of the enterprise after the death or disablement of her husband; the second is the ranch daughter who has rejected the traditional set of expectations for women in the region. These women do not represent a particular "family orientation", but vary among themselves. We find that widows are committed to continuity of kin control (as, for example, in "holding the operation together" until the son is old enough to operate it). However, all are ideologically committed to rural life and willing to defer consumption. They vary among themselves as to their intensity of focus upon the development of the enterprise, in some cases barely maintaining the enterprise; in other instances, actively engaged in developmental programs. They also vary in the degree of emphasis placed on the recreational aspect of ranching

In all cases, they are viewed by their neighbours as competent operators. The enterprises represent all levels of quality and productive capacity. The major similarity is that all have strong kin or quasi-kin ties with other households who are actively involved in work exchanges with them.

Summary

This chapter has focused on the style of participation in the enterprise by women, and the associated family orientations toward the enterprise, rural life, and toward educational achievement by their sons and daughters. All of these are important in the developmental process of young people and their perception of alternatives relevant for their own lives as adults.

We have seen that where the woman and the household focus their energies upon the development of the enterprise, no alternatives to agriculture are presented for their sons' consideration. Young men are caught up in the enterprise and, in essence, the boy becomes a major rationale for his father's continued development and expansion of the enterprise. Women are precluded from effective entrance into the agricultural occupation except as wife,[6] regardless of the household focus and the style of the mother's participation. Daughters, therefore, are obliged to consider alternatives which may take them out of the region. As stated earlier, many of these young women do not opt for another style of life, but instead marry early and, as a wife, enter agriculture through the back door.

Where the woman and the household centre their interest outside of the enterprise (either in cases where the enterprise is highly productive or where family satisfactions come from nonagricultural activities), then greater options are possible for both sons and daughters.

What is important, however, is the emphasis placed upon the pivotal position of the rural woman, both in the development of the

---

[6] This situation may change quite rapidly as the movement for a more equal opportunity structure for both men and women develops.

enterprise and in the social development of her children, a position which has for the most part gone unrecognized. Briefs presented in 1967 and 1968 to the Royal Commission on the Status of Women[7] took note of the fact that women do not acquire a legal share in the assets accruing from their participation in the family enterprise.[8]

The Saskatchewan Advisory Council on the Status of Women was established in January 1974, and began functioning in May of the same year. Reform of the Matrimonial Property Law was selected for immediate attention. This resulted in an amendment to the Married Women's Property Act (*Bill* 5).[9] This *Bill* — an interim measure to be in effect until the Law Reform Commission completes its study of marital property rights — gives to the court the "power to make a fair and equitable division of property between spouses".[10] The judge is directed to "take into account the respective contributions of the husband and wife whether in the form of money, services, prudent management, caring for the home and family or in any other form whatsoever."[11]

The final recommendations of the Law Reform Commission have yet to be completed and written into the laws of Saskatchewan. However, the first steps have been taken which provide juridical recognition for the important economic contribution of women in areas which have hitherto been ignored.

---

[7] *Report of the Royal Commission on the Status of Women in Canada, op. cit.*
[8] *Ibid.*, p. 43.
[9] Fifth Session, Seventeenth Legislature, Saskatchewan, *Bill* No. 5 of 1974-1975. An Act to amend The Married Women's Property Act. I am indebted to Margaret Harris for this data.
[10] *Ibid.*
[11] *Ibid.*

Supplementary Essay: A Comparison: Hutterite Women and Their Families

The Saskatchewan Cultural Ecology Research Program was committed to a comparative study of the differing adaptive styles and social organizations of all the significant social groups inhabiting the region. To date, these comparisons have dwelt chiefly on economic management and the use and allocation of resources (for examples, see Bennett, 1969-71, Chapter 10; Bennett, 1967, Chapter 9). Since Dr Kohl's book deals mainly with family relationships, and especially the role of women, we have an opportunity to deal comparatively with other matters. This appended chapter will emphasize the role of women in the society of the Hutterian Brethren who, since the early 1950s, have established several colonies in the Jasper region. The life of these colonies as of 1963-1965 has been described in a book and several articles (see references).

Since several good descriptive summaries of the Hutterian Brethren are available (Hostetler, 1974; Hostetler & Huntington, 1967; Peters, 1965), there will be no need for a detailed description of history and general culture. Hutterites are descendants of sixteenth-century Anabaptists, as are the Mennonites and Amish, which means that they have a heritage of Christian dissent from both Catholics and Protestants. Some elements of this dissenting position are shared with other Christian groups like the Quakers, Pentecostal sects, and Baptists (for example, pacifism; rejection of pastoral ordination and church centralization; baptism following adult confession of faith and moral readiness; and so on).

The most significant feature of Hutterian belief, however, consists of their dedication to the practice of communal property or "community of goods", as they call it. This is based on several passages in the Bible, most notably Acts 2:44-47, where the disciples of Jesus pooled their possessions and lived a communal and charitable existence. The underlying Hutterian sanction for the community of goods is not poverty, however, but rather the renunciation of acquisitiveness in the effort to reduce the sense of selfhood which is seen to impede a true expression of the spirit of the original Galilean Christian community. In some degree, this basic idea runs through all Christianity, but only dissenting, separatist groups have succeeded in implementing it. In the Catholic tradition, it was relegated to monasticism. In the Orient, the basic idea is also not unknown, as expressed in various monastic styles and mendicant orders. The Hutterian style is manifested in a reduction of personal possessions to a minimum, but with collective possessions permitted to expand to a reasonable level of comfort and security, always subject to definition by council.

Another Hutterian rationale for communal property is the control it provides over the physical and behavioural appearance of people, in order to present a living image of an egalitarian brotherhood, united in Christ. This goal can be achieved through uniformity of possessions, home-made clothing and, of course, a multitude of behavioural rules and regulations. Enforcement of the community of goods, insofar as it involves control over all expenditures and the pooling of all proceeds, requires nucleated settlement and a bureaucratic government. These settlements, essentially agricultural villages with features of an ancient European pattern, are called "colonies" in North America.

The institutional contrast between the Hutterian style of life and their neighbours in the Great Plains (where they all live) is especially strong, due to the emphatic professed individualism, private entrepreneurship, and nuclear familism of the non-Hutterian population. Moreover, the dispersed settlement pattern associated with this style, where the families live on widely separated small farms and ranches, offers a sharp contrast to the large buildings of the colony, huge gardens and grounds and its associated intense *Gemeinschaftliche* atmosphere. Some aspects of this contrast have been present throughout Hutterian history. However, at least in the European context, various communal aspects of village life, and the extensive cooperation characteristic of pre-industrial agriculture, provided more similarity between Hutterites and their neighbours.

Hutterian social structure, although featuring a notion of egalitarian brotherhood, is *de facto* patriarchal, being based on Biblical models. Men are considered to have the responsibility of leadership and authority, and are enjoined to cherish and protect women. Women are considered to be in charge of the domestic establishment; they do not have the right to vote in the colony assembly, although they do exert considerable behind-the-scenes influence on colony policies and financial expenditures. The colony instrumental structure (see diagram) is organized like a large diversified company, with a patriarchal executive echelon; a managerial stratum consisting of younger men; and a labour group consisting mainly of the youngest men and boys. Women constitute a distinct segment of the society, with a degree of instrumental hierarchy as indicated – the Garden Woman, Chief Cook, and so on. The chief authority figure in the colony is the First Minister – an elective position, like all Hutterian jobs, including those held by women. The Minister is the spiritual and moral leader of the colony – a "charismatic" figure in sociological jargon. However, in actuality a colony is an exceedingly complex power and authority system with much give-and-take and complicated, ever-changing exchange relationships. Hutterites recognize the contradictory synthesis of egalitarian democracy and patriarchal hierarchism characteristic of their system, and have a detailed philosophical rationale for it. Here, as in so many other facets of Hutterian life, there is awareness of the extreme difficulty for human beings to live in the pure Christian way of total love and brotherhood. Compromises must be made because humans are not perfect; they can only approximate Christ's message. As Hutterites would put it, the lot of man – and woman – is especially hard because to live in a Christian way takes constant effort and endless discipline. The fate of Christian man is to suppress imperfect selfhood, which constantly falls away from God; yet, in order to attain social continuity, humans must tolerate a degree of individual difference, authority, and competition.

The Hutterian occupation of the Jasper region began in 1952 with the first colony moving eastward into the drier country from Alberta. The first three colonies all bought land east of Jasper town, up to the Alberta line, where farmers of central and eastern European stock had difficulties transmitting the enterprises to their sons because of the small and uneconomic size of these units. The colonies moving into Saskatchewan were part of the orderly process of fission which characterizes the Hutterian econocology: when colonies reach a population magnitude of about a hundred and thirty persons, they begin planning for a division, the first step of which is the purchase of land for the "new farm", as most colonies call the future colony site. After this farm is brought into cultivation and basic buildings constructed, the parent colony draws lots and half of the population moves to the new site, where the process of economic build-up begins once again. By 1973,

Formal Organization of the Hutterian Colony

(All adults baptized males take part in the Assembly—the colony's group-decision body. Women do not participate or vote.)

GOVERNING ROLES

ELDERS, AUFSEHERN, OR CHIEF EXECUTIVES OF THE COLONY

1. **Church Elder or First Minister**
(Spiritual leader; communications officer)
(Most colonies have a second minister)

2. **Householder or Colony Boss**
(Business manager; financial officer)

3. **Farm Boss**
(Personnel director; crops manager)

4. **German Teacher**
(Teacher; mediator; counsellor; often a second minister. Not always an executive—must be voted in. Often the Gardener.)

Additional Elders or Councillors
(Semi-retired men not in executive jobs.)

(Authority principle: *primus inter pares*, but with slight graduation as represented by 1, 2, 3, 4.)

COUNCIL, OR VORSTEHEN DER GEMEINDE

(Made up of Elders, Aufsehern, or Chief Executives, in both elective and honorary positions.)
Membership: 4 Chief Executives; Councillors; plus 2 or 3 Farm Enterprise Managers, as below;

AGRICULTURAL MANAGEMENT ROLES

FARM ENTERPRISE MANAGERS (elective)
(Any number; varies with enterprise.)

| Cattle (beef) | Swine | Sheep | Chickens, Eggs | Ducks, Geese | → Crops | → Garden |

Technical:
Blacksmith
Mechanic
Carpenter
Shoemaker
Etc.

(Authority: Over particular enterprises only—no graduation; no group organization)

LABOUR FORCE

A. **Labourers**
(All men 15 years or older not in executive or managerial positions. When baptized, in voting group.)

B. **All Men in Executive-Managerial Roles**
(When available, or on call.)

C. **All Women**
(Especially younger, unmarried.)

Women Do Not Vote or Participate in Assembly

FEMALE HIERARCHY

Head Cook
(Only executive position for women—not elective)

Garden Women
School Woman
Kindergarten Woman

(Workers, usually spinsters, rotate in jobs.)

↓

All Other Women

Reprinted from John W. Bennett, *Hutterian Brethren: The Agricultural Economy and Social Organization of a Communal People* (Stanford: Stanford University Press, 1967), p. 144.

eight fission-halves of Alberta colonies had appeared in the Jasper region. Jasper Hutterites consider this to be the ceiling, since the colonies are aware of possible destructive competition if they become too numerous in a given region. By 1973, some of the early-1950s entrants were beginning to plan for their own fission, and sites elsewhere in Saskatchewan and Montana were being considered.

The Life Cycle: Childhood

Hutterian children are raised communally, but up to the age of three they are "house children", living entirely with their parents and cared for jointly by parents and older siblings – when the latter are not at school or performing chores. From three to five, children spend most of the day away from parents, in the colony kindergarten or *Kleinschul.* At six, they move into the *Grossschul* or "German School", as it is usually called in English. From six to fifteen they also attend public elementary school on the colony premises, taught by an outside schoolteacher assigned by the local school board. Therefore, when the child leaves the toddler stage, most of the effective disciplinary socialization, in addition to schooling, is administered by adults other than parents. The pattern is similar to the kibbutz,* although Hutterian children always sleep in the parental apartment, and the colony does not have a residential nursery or boarding school. However, from kindergarten on, children eat in a separate communal dining room, away from the adult dining hall.

Sex differences in behaviour and training appear gradually. Certainly by the age of three, sex differences in experience are apparent: the little girls accompany their mothers in the domestic chores around the apartment, the communal kitchen and dining hall, laundry, or garden; while the boys follow their fathers on their jobs around the farm and shops. Still, one of the most common colony sights is a pack of children of both sexes, aged three to six, running around the colony in exploratory play, often shepherded by an older girl. In the kindergarten, sex-role differences are observed: the girls at one end, playing with dolls and utensils; the boys at the other, with blocks, vehicle toys, and the like. This pattern merges by age seven into appropriate chores: girls will be assigned kitchen duties; boys will help their fathers. The general pattern, except for the important difference in group socialization and supervision by a larger adult cadre, does not differ significantly from that observed for the non-Hutterian farm and ranch families.

The peer group autonomy of Hutterian children, noticeable to the colony visitor who sees groups of both sexes and various ages up to

---

* For a comparison of the Hutterian colony and the Israeli kibbutz, see Barkin & Bennett (1972).

fifteen is a matter of considerable interest. There is no question that up to age fifteen, Hutterian boys and girls function largely as equals, with considerable free conversation and give-and-take, despite the growing separation of tasks. Young adolescent girls seem to function in two worlds: the women are teaching them the postures of submission and domesticity, while their behaviour with boys of their own age is quite free and egalitarian. Hutterites believe that this period of freedom and equality is needed in order to cement the basic bonds of brotherhood, to give the young person experience in true Christian equality before he must make the necessary compromises with the world – that is, the differentiated colony system. Moreover, this period of adolescent mingling is expected to work out key social attitudes and relationships that will transfer on into adulthood; that is, into the next generation in control of the colony or its daughter colony.

A third reason for encouraging these peer group associations is to assist in the dilution of sibling solidarity. This is so because while the nuclear family is the basic kinship unit of Hutterian society, as it is for their neighbours, it is also a constant threat to the solidarity of the colony, the commune. Hutterites rely on the family for stability and love, but they also need to control the tendencies toward factionalism which over-solidaristic and rivalrous nuclear kin groups frequently generate. Sibling solidarity is extremely strong in Hutterian society – hardly surprising, since families are unusually large: ten children was the mean a couple of decades ago. Brothers constitute groups who will assume managerial, and eventually, executive positions in the colony; there is a natural tendency, which must be controlled, to seek these positions as a bloc, or to vote as a bloc in the colony assembly on various issues. Sisters have similar bloc tendencies, although the women lack the political instrumentalities to make their weight felt in a formal sense. Brothers and sisters have lifelong ties; they commonly aspire to exchange marriages with brothers and sisters in another colony, creating an expanded nuclear-affinal group within the colony (Hutterites have patrilocal residence).

Hence the peer group formations are expected to assist in the countering of excessive sibling solidarity by providing the opportunity for young people from different nuclear groups to form friendships and alliances. Adults look on this with approval, since it is good for the colony, but there may be ambivalence if, for example, a son or daughter forms a close friendship with a peer from a nuclear family which has strained relationships with their own. Hutterian social life has a dense texture of this type of interaction; male-female role relationships of young people are inextricably fused with power relationships which have their significance for the future stability and functioning of colony and kinship society. The pattern is that of a nucleated small village populated by kin, usually one large extended family. Non-Hutterian

Jasperites can more easily control their kinship relationships due to the dispersed settlement patterns. However, there are some situations where – when several sisters all retired in the same small town – we find something approximating the colony social atmosphere.

At age fifteen the Hutterite young person is considered a functional adult: boys and girls move into the adult dining room, taking positions at the foot of the tables (as they age and assume responsibility, they move up in seniority position). No ceremony marks this assumption of adulthood; it is not until around the age of twenty that the Hutterite makes his significant passage into the Christian brotherhood, when he requests baptism. In other words, between fifteen and about twenty, the young person is in a kind of limbo – a transitional era during which he is expected to manifest erratic and often disloyal symptoms. Young men can leave the colony and work on the outside for a year or two if they insist. This option is barred to the girls, however, and in its place there develop rather conspicuous bands of late teenage girls who form cliques – to some extent a prolongation of the pre-fifteen groups, although the boys are less evident now. Both boys and girls in this critical five-year span constitute apprentice adults – not only with respect to colony traditions and lifeways, but also for jobs and duties. The group is a kind of "mobile labor force" (Hostetler 1974, p. 222), available for any and all tasks, and out of these casual assignments will come permanent skills and interests. Just as social ties are forged in the pre-fifteen years, so too the responsibility skills and working relationships are created in the pre-baptismal years. (Likewise, the rebelliousness, oat-sowing experiences of the young men.)

These pre-baptismal years also see the beginning of courtship. Because colonies are usually full of close kin, more than half of all Hutterites find mates outside the colony – often in the same colonies which then become linked in large bilateral affinal networks (Bennett 1967, Chapter 5). The "mobile labor force" is often trucked to other colonies for work and visits, and on these occasions the young people will form friendship cliques and "dating", as Hutterite young people now call it, may result. The same can occur in the home colony as well, but only between young people who are not too closely related or who are approved by the parents and the uncles and aunts. Although Hutterites control the movement of their young people and adults rigorously – private automobiles, for example, are not allowed – there is a surprising amount of autonomy of movement and mild cheating of the system (evening hikes down the road to the next colony; sneaking an occasional ride with an indulgent relative), to produce a good deal of courtship and mingling among the young. The adults know this goes on, although they will deny it to outsiders, preferring to give an impression of stern control. This pre-baptismal period is also expected to be one of exploration of the Outside and its pleasures: secret transistor radios, comic books, wrist watches, arranging to have visitors and town acquaintances take photographs, and so on. Girls may secrete small vials of perfume, dime-store jewelry and the like. In a communal society with strict sumptuary regulations every person is expected to have a private hiding place or strongbox, absolutely barred to others, taken out only to show to intimates. Girls as well as boys have these; it is a secret world of marginal individuality, and it provides the person with the language and meanings of the larger society, even though it may never go beyond this stage.*

Viewing the pattern of socialization comparatively, we can say that while the basic themes of childhood experience and its kinship matrix are broadly similar in Hutterian and non-Hutterian society in Jasper, the details are very different. There is, first, the intensive training in the Hutterian *Gemeinschaft*: the requirements for constant interactive adjustment and the corresponding need to suppress much of what is considered "individuality" by the outside. There is, in addition, extensive training in a much larger variety of tasks: the manifold activities of the colony offer a wider set of experiences in the agricultural, mechanical, and domestic spheres than is usually available to the boy or girl growing up on a farm or ranch. The experiences do not differ in kind, but in scope and degree: a farm daughter may have one or two younger siblings to care for part of the time, the Hutterite girl will have at least four and will also be required to help out with the younger children of her several aunts, sisters-in-law, and friends. Hutterian children have constant associations with peers in large numbers; the typical Jasper child will experience something comparable only at intervals, and usually only at school. Hutterite children live surrounded by adults who constantly educate, admonish, train, and punish strictly. While the Jasper child's network of kin serves as a social control mechanism, its impact is much less. In John Hostetler's study of adolescent attitudes, he found that Hutterite children show much less fear of adults than the non-Hutterite farm children; the study also showed that Hutterite children expect punishment as a matter of routine; the other children resented and feared it [Hostetler (1974), p. 227].

The Life Cycle: Marriage and Adulthood

Baptism is the most significant social rite in Hutterian life. It is considered to be a formal manifestation of what Hutterites call *Gelassenheit*, a word which means composure or collectedness, but which in Hutterian rhetoric refers to self-submission or giving-upness;

---

* For test data on Hutterian adolescent attitudes, as compared with non-Hutterian children, see Hostetler (1974), pp. 226ff. This is based on an unpublished study made in South Dakota.

– in this case, surrender to Christ. And since Christ – the church – is equated with the colony existence, it is *living* in the Christian way, since Hutterites do not distinguish between "going to church" and everyday existence. That is, when the young person is ready to accept baptism, it signifies readiness to be a Hutterite, and this means a willingness to give up the "foolishness" of the earlier years and, above all, to accept the institutionalized roles of the society.

For the girls, this means acceptance of what outsiders view as second-class status. As already noted, women lack the vote, and must leave the assembly (usually held after church services) before colony policies are discussed. They must accept an unending round of domestic tasks, including fairly hard labour, like painting and varnishing, the laundry, operating the large food-processing machinery, and long hours in the colony garden and in the communal kitchen. However, in one role context the Hutterite and Jasper young women share similar expectations: leaving home for marriage. The majority of Hutterite girls leave the colony because of the shortage of potential mates inside, and because Hutterites practice patrilocal marriage residence. Hutterite young men stay home – although they will eventually move to a new branch colony of the home colony – and this resembles the farm or ranch son's occasional establishment of his own enterprise. The girl knows that she will have to learn a new social world – not especially "new" in the sense of culture shock since Hutterian life is remarkably uniform, but certainly new in the sense of coping with a fresh set of relatives. Only Hutterite women have this experience: that of becoming a link between two sets of kin, and in most cases, between two colonies. These linkages are crucial; they are not only social, but usually involve important economic exchanges as well. This is an important role, and Hutterites are well aware of it; they place considerable responsibility in the new bride's hands, since they look to her as a way of establishing new ties and profitable relationships – and in this sense her status is "high", not "low", in Hutterian society.

There is a similarity here with the non-Hutterite female role: like the Hutterite girl, the Jasper daughter who marries into a distant community will be expected to provide a link into another set of in-law ties which may have significant consequences – if not always economically, at least in the sense of providing friendships or "places to stay" or visit.

Marriage, as we have noted, is preceded by courtship – Hutterian marriages are not, in any formalized sense, "arranged". However, in general, there is less freedom of movement and mate-selection than occurs on the Outside. Marriage can take place only after a careful analysis of the situation by the parents, uncles, and aunts, and the ministers and other officials of the two colonies involved. The couple are under no illusion that the union is entirely of their own making: their marriage is a junction between two collectivities. Only in some of the large family ranching enterprises in Jasper will marriage approximate this degree of social involvement. That is, the pattern is not alien to Jasper, but it appears only where the social magnitudes begin to resemble those of the colony.

Although there are some similarities between the large ranching families and the colony, due to comparable numbers of siblings and kinship network size, the quality of social relationships within the family unit is very different. Hutterian society is a conflict-avoiding, love-maximizing system in which quarrels between siblings, and offspring and parents, are suppressed, and, of course, diluted by the large number of relatives involved in everyday, face-to-face interaction. However, the large family ranches, as Dr Kohl has shown, are characterized by frequent open quarrels, sudden departures of one or more sons, rivalry and bickering between sons and father, and so on. Lacking the ideological restraints of the Christian brotherhood, and lacking clear institutional solutions to succession (or rather, in the case of the colony, automatic socioeconomic-demographic continuity due to collective ownership), the individual large family enterprise inevitably experiences a good deal of social conflict and unpredictability.

The position of the young bride in the colony of her husband resembles the classic situation described for Japanese women: she is under the control of her mother-in-law and is "on the spot", so to speak. While Hutterian life is, as noted, remarkably uniform, each colony has its own little differences and styles, and the very uniformity means that Hutterites place emphasis on these marginal differences. The new wife must learn them (not a difficult task) and she must seek information primarily from her husband, since his mother generally considers that the daughter-in-law is on trial. She watches her, rather than coaches. Even so, the Hutterites take pains to relieve this burden: the conjugal bedroom is known as the new wife's room – not her husband's – and she is encouraged to take charge of the domestic establishment. She has been carefully schooled by her own mother for this type of responsibility, and the majority of young wives seem to handle the job adequately and without undue stress. Moreover, Hutterian socialization teaches people to suppress anxiety and grief – to stand on their own feet and do their best for the collectivity. On Jasper farms and ranches the young wife may or may not have to cope with her mother-in-law; this is variable, depending on residential patterns and other factors – just as succession and continuity in the family enterprise is variable and hard to predict. The Hutterian system, on the other hand, is eminently predictable, and its participants are well prepared for the tasks and roles.

As among other Christian bodies, and especially fundamentalists, sexual relations are a tabooed subject (although in the "foolish years" of pre-baptism the teenage boys and girls may tell mildly dirty jokes and make suggestive remarks). But informants insist there is no formal instruction in sexual relations, and no explicit training of the young girl to be attractive to men. Male-female relationships are assimilated into the frame of the collectivity: what a woman does with her husband is private, but its consequences – the bearing of children – are the routine public business of the colony and are to be carried on with a minimum of fuss. The large families help: when a woman has a child, one or more of her sisters in the colony or from her home colony will visit and help her over the first two or three weeks. The baby is given much affection and delighted attention. Whatever her mother-in-law may think of her, if the wife produces children at regular intervals she has done her primary duty to the colony and to the Christian brotherhood.

All this is in contrast to the Jasper situation, where the nuclear families produce children with only variable and generally weak reference to larger social units. Bearing children is usually not a duty, but a chore, an opportunity, an adventure – whatever it might be for the particular couple – and, occasionally, in the large enterprise clans without a male heir, something approximating the Hutterite context of duty.

Not all women marry. Authoritative data is lacking, but the average colony will have about five spinsters. These are women who have elected to stay in the home colony and not marry: they serve useful and important roles, and Hutterites take note of the fact that no special compulsion is placed on women to marry. Spinsters supervise the kindergarten, direct the female labour, and take care of widower fathers and uncles in their old age. There is nothing comparable to this in Jasper. A spinster is a woman without a role, although a few become schoolteachers (really the only function an unmarried woman can have in this society). Even so, Hutterite spinsters are more often than not rather lonely, eccentric people; nearly every colony has one or two such women who in their old age become victims of the Hutterian depressive psychoses, of which more later.

A Hutterite friend of the writer's once remarked that "this life is just one big retirement scheme". The aged in Hutterian society simply phase out of routine tasks – there is no formalized retirement decision. A man or woman simply works as long as he or she can, and gives up jobs that are too arduous or complex. The aged are respected – old men become generalized Elders who advise the colony executives and provide an aura of wisdom. This is no sham; in a traditional society the aged really do have wisdom: they have seen many things, they know the alternatives and the consequences, and while young people occasionally make mild fun of them, there is genuine respect and affection. In Hutterian society there is no "problem" about retirement of the father from the enterprise, as in Jasper farms and ranches. There is no extra expense associated with financing the old couple's retirement home in town – which has become such a burden for young Jasper agriculturalists. The aged in Hutterian society are often given little ceremonial tasks; many of the old men become bread slicers, sitting at the head of the table, put in charge of the large loaves of crusty bread and of other dishes that require sharing. The old woman is the first to kiss the new baby, and she is consulted as to the details of caring for it. Old women are known in many colonies as informal guardians of the faith: they are frequently the most devout Hutterites, and the Minister will call attention to their piety.

Role Dualism

Dr Kohl has emphasized the duality of the female role in Jasper: the woman is the domestic executive and labourer, but is also informally expected to contribute significantly to the operation and financing of the enterprise by assisting her husband, making use of her generally superior education, and controlling domestic expenditures and investments in order to allow for enterprise development. How does this compare with the situation of the Hutterite woman?

There are both similarities and differences. Hutterite women have, perhaps, a more formalized role assignment as domestics than have the Jasper women, due to the ideology and also to the sheer magnitude of the task. The Hutterian domestic establishment is much larger and more complex, since more people are involved and since there is self-sufficiency in many foodstuffs (more gardening, food processing, storage, and so on). Moreover, Hutterite women make the clothes for everyone in the colony, in addition to maintaining the family apartments. In general, the female tasks resemble those of an agricultural village community of the pre-industrial age; there is no time for club memberships, card parties, benefits, and all the other activities the Jasper women indulge in. The Hutterite woman is of the colony, not of the world; she lives in a self-contained system. If she wishes to read and train her mind, she will have to do it with the help of her husband or not at all, and very few women manage to do it. She has almost no opportunity to form friendships with non-Hutterian women – in contrast to many Hutterite men, who do strike up friendships with farmers, ranchers, merchants, and local politicians.

Moreover, the distinction between the domestic world and the colony economic world is quite sharp. The Hutterite woman is an official member of the domestic establishment; her husband belongs to the colony instrumentality. The woman has no legitimate access to her husband's world of crops, markets, and machines. However, this is not quite reciprocal: the men have access to the domestic sphere in the sense of being in charge of its financing and retaining the power to grant the requests of the women for investments in it. Thus, to some extent, the Jasper pattern is reversed: in the latter, the wife has informal access to the enterprise; while in the colony, the husband has informal access to the domestic establishment. The situation may be charted as follows:

	Domestic Establishment	Enterprise
Hutterite women	Major and official role	No significant role
Hutterite man	Informal control and participation	Major and official role
Jasper woman	More or less major and recognized role	Often important, but not officially recognized role
Jasper man	Highly variable, and informal role	Major and officially recognized role

This chart shows that the patterns have nuances of difference set within a general frame of basic similarity. The differences are perhaps more important than the similarities from the standpoint of what may be called "life chances": the Hutterian woman has considerably fewer than her counterpart in Jasper society, because she is barred from free participation in the Outside, and because her domestic responsibilities are multifarious and heavy. She has, in general, fewer opportunities to participate actively in the enterprise, since the colony economy is under the control of the men, who have the right to discuss and vote on policy. Yet the Hutterite woman can influence things behind the scenes by working on her husband. When the women decide to exert joint pressure, they can usually get their way. However, they lack the intimate familiarity with the enterprise found among most Jasper farm housewives.

The chief factors behind similarities and differences are, of course, the following: first, the ideology of women as different from, and dependent upon, men. This is overt and formal in the colony; in Jasper, it may lie behind the scenes, as a general Christian understanding, but the reality of the democratic nuclear family partnership system has all but eliminated it as a principle of role behaviour. It survives primarily in the institutions of property ownership and responsibility.

Second, the existence of the colony as a village milieu in which women must function. The Jasper farm housewife is isolated; the Hutterian housewife is surrounded by kin and nonkin. The Hutterite woman is a member of a large socioeconomic establishment and a living human birth-to-death community. While the Jasper farmwife is subject to social pressure, she can withdraw to her private world on the enterprise.

Third is the common influence of an agricultural occupation. Both Hutterite and Jasper women live in a farming milieu, which confers many similarities in experience and outlook. Still, there are differences: while Jasper women are more knowledgeable about prices and markets, and usually can operate one or more of the big farm machines, Hutterite women are better informed about vegetable gardening, orchards, and food preparation and preservation; both are essential to the agrarian life, but each represents a different section of that life. Both roles are functional in the agricultural round, and both have a common heritage in the history of Western civilization. Translating into general behavioural terms, Hutterite women perceive Jasper women as aggressive and forward; Jasper women view Hutterite women as submissive and overworked.

Perhaps, in the last analysis, the source of the most significant difference between these two sets of women is the exposure to urban standards. Jasper women are connected to the world of consumption, and follow its styles and rhetoric. Hutterian women have little or no contact with this world; they wander through the variety stores in Jasper town on their once-a-month-or-so trip to town, viewing the gewgaws and gadgets and pretty clothes with a dazed expression. In the eyes of a Jasper housewife who happens to witness it, the Hutterite woman appears exotic, pitiful, beyond the pale – and never the twain shall meet.

Change and Transition

Hutterian *society* changes very slowly – only marginally – while Hutterian *economy* adapts easily and efficiently to changes in the means and ends of production. Hutterian institutions represent a revitalized creation dating from the 1870s; before the removal to North America, the sect had been in a period of decline, and communal property and the commune system generally had been in a state of dissolution. Hutterites are, in a word, uptight, because they have reason to fear a recurrence of difficulty; all communal societies undergo them, and even though the Hutterian system has proved more durable than most, it is not invulnerable. Consequently, Hutterites are extremely cautious about innovation, especially in the behavioural sphere.

However, in the nineteen-sixties and seventies there were signs of change, and many of these changes principally concerned the women (Bennett 1975). The key words are *affluence* and *consumption*. The remarkable success of the Hutterian economic system in adapting to the high-cost, high-returns grain-livestock production system of the Western Prairies has provided them with a growing surplus. Much of this surplus is used in the financing of new branch colonies, but many older colonies have begun to invest their money in comforts and conveniences. These are always collective; there is no evidence of increasing personal consumption, because the colonies continue to disperse very small amounts of spending money.

Many, if not most, of these consumption gains are the fruits of concerted campaigns by the women to make their lives easier. In the decade 1960-1970, the Jasper colonies began to install indoor plumbing, with private bathrooms for each of the nuclear family apartments in the row houses; vinyl-covered floors and walls; and processed siding on the houses, the school, and the kitchen-dining hall building. Electric floor polishers became the rule, with each wife receiving one; basement "rec rooms" began to be common under the apartments, and cement sidewalks, expanses of green lawn and carefully controlled flower beds made their appearance. Interior decor began to emerge: women were insisting on fancier curtains, plastic flowers on the chest of drawers, coloured bedspreads and, in many colonies, "party dresses" for the toddler girls, bought at the village dry goods stores and discount stores in the larger towns, made a cautious appearance. Central propane or electric baseboard heating became a standard convenience in all newly built colonies, and many of the old began installing them as well.

More subtle and potentially much more important changes may be signified by a decrease in the number of children born.* Families were stopping at six, instead of nine children, and there was little doubt that these were primarily decisions of the women supported, or at least not opposed, by the younger husbands, who are aware of the fact that Hutterites in Western Canada are beginning to find an end to the profitable expansion in the more productive parts of Alberta and Saskatchewan due to shortage of land and community resistance.

In short, a quiet – very quiet – revolution in the assertiveness of Hutterite women has been taking place in the colonies and it can be expected to continue. Hutterites are cultural separatists, but only to a point. There is no absolute insulation from the Outside, and Hutterite women are increasingly aware of the demands North American women have made for a greater share in the system. One consequence will be greater variation in the role of women – and of men – from colony to colony. This is already noticeable in the two branches of the sect – the Lehrer Leut and the Darius Leut – represented in the Jasper region. The Darius have always been more tolerant of behavioural individuality than the Lehrer; in recent years Darius women, especially young women, have seemingly been permitted to prolong the "foolish years" into young wifehood. One sees Darius girls and young women with more carefully tailored and fitted garments, and an occasional trace of lipstick or powder. Postures often seem more feminine and pliant, fabrics for the women's dresses a bit finer or off-standard. These are all

---

* Childbirth takes place in the Regional Hospital where birth control information is available.

marginalia, but considering the powerful constraints in the system, they are of the utmost importance because they signify a rise in feminine self-esteem. The changes are not yet visible, at the time of writing, among the Lehrer women, and the Lehrer generally are the most "uptight" of the three *leute* (the third, the Schmiede, are represented in Manitoba only).

The consumption gains for women could have important psychological effects. There exist a few older studies of Hutterite personality which, although inadequate by contemporary standards of research, do provide some insight into the psychic costs of Hutterian life. In general, Hutterites were found to have quite good mental health, that is, in more contemporary terms, they appear to make good adjustments to their own constrained social system. Both women and men show the usual symptoms of neurotic conflicts, but these do not appear to be greater than for any other human population, including the Jasper. The objects or causes of conflict may, of course, be somewhat different due to cultural differences.

Psychotic reactions among Hutterites, however, constitute a special problem. The rate of psychosis is probably no higher than in the general society, but the relative rates of types of psychosis, and of men and women, appear to differ [see Kaplan and Plaut (1956) for data]. In the first place, the most common psychotic illness among Hutterites is a depressive state called by the Brethren *Anfechtung* (literally, "temptation" by the Devil). This is more common than schizoid symptoms – a possible reversal of the tendency in the general North American population. Secondly, depressive illness is more common among Hutterian women than among men – another reversal of the distribution in the general population. Depressive states are precisely what one would expect to find in Hutterian society, because psychiatrists have found that "manic-depressive" illness is most common among close, interactive, familial-type groups. And so far as the women are concerned, one might anticipate that they would show a higher incidence since they are the most cloistered of Hutterites; the men have far more opportunity to mingle with people on the Outside.

Comparing the situation with Jasper women, it may be recalled that in Chapters VI and VII, Dr Kohl commented on some mental health data in the form of case protocols based on referrals from the Jasper region to the Saskatchewan mental health program. She noted that women were more common than men in the two case samples from 1960 and 1970, but that the number of women declined by 10 percent between the two ends of the decade, reflecting the improvement in the opportunities women have in Jasper for movement and gratification.

These findings may bear some comparison with the Hutterian case. There is a similar tendency for women to be more emotionally concerned than men; perhaps agrarian life in a difficult environment is especially hard on women, regardless of social organization or culture. And secondly, there is the suggestion of a change for the healthier in the important decade of economic development and prosperity in Jasper. While we have no case data available for Hutterite women, our observations suggest that the increase in self-assertiveness and general outgoingness during the decade, and apparently associated with consumption gains in the colonies, instigated by women, is something comparable to that noted for Jasper women generally.

Little fundamental change in Hutterite life can be expected so long as basic institutions remain the same. Hutterite women cannot be expected to assume the roles of farm and ranch women while the colony remains what it is: a large, diversified enterprise devoted to a high degree of self-sufficiency and requiring a substantial labour input from the women in order to maintain this style. If further change does take place, it will be in the direction of a more relaxed personal style for the women – surely the system can stand this without serious consequences. One might also hazard the prediction that in a generation Hutterite women will also obtain the right to vote in the assembly, especially on issues affecting the domestic establishment, although it must be admitted that the recent consumption changes are proof that they can get their way even without the vote. If Hutterite women ever open communication with their alternates on the farms and ranches, this might well have important consequences. For the time being, however, Hutterian life is unique, a world apart, an alternative style and a successful one. It has expectant social and human costs, but the evidence suggests these costs are bearable, especially when they are targets of one of the most efficient socialization systems human society has devised. Hutterite women are the backbone of this system; their accomplishments deserve the utmost respect.

Appendix: Methods of Research

As in any social situation, one's friendship, kinship, work, and association ties delineate social space for individuals. The understanding of these social networks is necessary to understand the processes of social life. In the study of a sparse, dispersed population, it is not possible (as it is in the nucleated villages so frequently studied by anthropologists) to sit in the centre of the community and observe the totality of social life. Social life is based upon spheres of activity – work, kinship, neighbourhood, shared interests, and formal voluntary associations – which establish social fields or social relationships for any given individual. These social ties have their own geographical areas, thus allowing one to define social boundaries in physical terms.

The differing histories of ranching and farming occupations provide the background for different geographical-social patterns. The economic stability and longer residence of the ranching families has meant that there are multiple kin connections between ranchers throughout the region. The two modes of production require different work patterns, with consequent different rhythms to social life. Different vested interests in the market apparatuses of livestock and grain farming set different associational ties (although these were merging during the research decade, as farmers developed their cattle business), all of which make for different social networks for the two occupational and social groups. Even though there are many ties of kinship, friendship, and association which link the two occupational groups, social boundaries are still maintained.

Entrance into social networks requires establishment of social ties with one or several members involved in the network. My contacts with the ranching social network were made possible through a stay with a ranch family who introduced me to the rancher's world throughout the region. Thus it was possible to interview family members of nearly all of the ranch enterprises in the region. Not only were they relatively few in number (a total of thirty-two enterprises), but the many interconnecting social and kin ties meant that supplementary information about others in the same social network could be gathered on any one visit.

There was no similar regional society of farmers, since they maintained a geographically narrower network of social ties based primarily upon the area served by the old district school houses or the small town. It therefore became necessary to rely on sample populations of farmers. Initially, the Canada Census of Agriculture categories on income and production were used to establish a sample population for the first major interviewing project in 1962 and 1963. This initial stratified sample covered the entire region, but did not offer the proper sources for information on social networks. We then decided to choose "specimen" townships[1] (see Map I) for intensive studies of enterprise and family. These townships comprise the geographic heartland of the Jasper region as we defined it.

The township unit was chosen since many categories of economic, demographic, and land tenure data were available for that unit from at least 1900. The selection of the original ten townships (in 1970, two more were added) out of a total of a hundred and twenty townships was based on the following characteristics:

1. The Embassy farming township included both straight grain and cattle-grain farming. Since it was distant (forty miles) from Jasper, the villages of Embassy and Eldora were important service centres for these farmers. It has been heavily homesteaded with a subsequent sharp decline in population, and thus was typical of those areas with a large number of abandoned farmsteads.

2. The Jasper Town farming township was chosen since it was close to the town of Jasper and offered a contrast to the Embassy farmers in terms of social participation in town activities.

3. The Ranching specimen township is in effect three townships

[1] The region consists of some one hundred and twenty townships, each thirty-six square miles, a result of the original land survey made for the allocation of homesteads.

which are geographically coterminous and which include a majority of the ranchers in the Cypress Hills.

4. The three townships around Happydale and the two at Greenfields were chosen to provide additional material on migration and enterprise – succession dynamics. The former had retained its population and had a high percentage of succession from father to son; the latter, once a heavily homesteaded area, had lost most of its population.

5. Two townships near Sunrise and Altheim were added in 1970 to extend the geographical scope of the study of family and enterprise.

Members of the homesteading generation were interviewed in order to develop a history of homestead settlement for each specimen township. Subsequently, the remaining family enterprise members were interviewed. Others, outside of the specimen townships, were also included. Since the research continued for a decade, the sample populations changed as the life cycle of the enterprise household changed: operators either retired and moved to towns or died; their places were then sold or divided or their sons took over. Thus, the sample of households changed over time. The initial sample of agricultural family enterprise households, what we called the "1960 sample of contemporary operators in control", consisted of 127 households: seventy-eight were farming enterprises (defining themselves as farmers even in the six cases where their total income came from cattle) and thirty-two were ranching enterprises (two of whom earned more than half of their income from the sale of wheat). In subsequent years this initial sample was modified. There were additional family interviews in the Sunrise and Altheim townships. These, plus the natural increase in younger couples who succeeded to parental enterprises, and the natural decrease due to death and retirement changed the sample to one hundred and thirty-nine households. Unless otherwise noted, this is the population on which the generalizations discussed in this book are based.

The history of the family and development of the enterprise was obtained by writing the family genealogy, which also mapped the kinship and marriage connections within the region. For the most part, these genealogies begin with the family's entrance into the district, not because this is the point at which the informant begins his lineage, but because of the interests of the study. The genealogies were not collected for a formal kinship study aimed at delineating the total universe of kin, but rather the major interest lay in the instrumental and integrative functions of the kinship network within a particular habitat. In addition to mapping the kinship connections within the region, this method enabled the collection of migration data for two and, in some cases, three generations. Information about attitudes toward occupation choices and past life history experiences as well as data on attitudes toward the outside community were also obtained. Perhaps most important, the collection of genealogies served as a useful and quick means of obtaining a perspective on regional social systems, and serendipitously supplemented the sparse census data for the early years.

Traditional anthropological field methods were used; that is, participant observation in community social affairs and family affairs, and informal visiting. Official records such as land tenure maps, school and health records, historical documents, and the regional newspaper formed the background of general field note material. However, the long interviews held with household members are the most important source of information in the sociological study.

Because people placed the interview situation in the category of "visiting", the interview (with few exceptions) offered an opportunity for informal talk and observation of family relationships in a relaxed situation. The sparse population and the interconnecting social networks of friendship and kinship made it possible to meet the same people in different social situations, for example, in another person's home, at a picnic, in town or school, and so on.

The interviews centred around family roles and obligations, the socialization of, and expectations for, children, and the history of the family enterprise. Since the interviews usually extended into the meal hour, fathers and children were present and all participated – sometimes disagreeing with one another – thereby providing an excellent means for observing differences in the same household as well as identifying issues to be raised with one or another of the household members at other times.

Participation with other field workers[2] made it possible to compare notes and check perceptions and information. Furthermore, as men, they were privy to areas of social life where I, as a woman, could not enter. Their presence in the same situation highlighted the different expectations for men and women, despite the fact that we shared the role of researcher.

Within the past eight years there have been many personal accounts of the field work process.[3] What emerges in reading these accounts is the variation and indeterminability of each situation. Peggy Golde[4] has abstracted five recurring themes particularly relevant to women field workers: issues of protection and vulnerability; initial suspicion; conformity to the norms of the community; reciprocity; and culture shock. These are issues which were relevant, if not as dramatic as other field work experiences, in my own situation.

---

[2] These were John W. Bennett; Charles Thomas; Neils Braroe; Les Potter; Ivan Clark; and Lyle Dunwald. The last three were residents of the Jasper region.

[3] See, for example, D. G. Jongmans and P. C. W. Gutkind, eds., *Anthropologists in the Field* (New York: Humanities Press, 1967); Morris Freilich, ed., *Marginal Natives: Anthropologists at Work* (New York: Harper and Row, 1970); Peggy Golde, ed., *Women in the Field* (Chicago: Aldine Publishing Co., 1970); and Rosalie Wax, *Doing Fieldwork: Warnings and Advice* (Chicago: University of Chicago Press, 1971).

[4] *Op. cit.*, p. 5.

The most relevant factor in providing ease of entry was the fact that I was a married woman with children. The role of mother and wife I shared with my informants established me as part of the woman's society. I had immediate credentials to discuss "women's" topics. This, I feel, made my initial entrance into the lives of Jasperites easier than it was for the male researchers whose occupations of teaching and research were outside those occupational skills required for agriculture.[5]

The fact that Jasper is not the isolated jungle of New Guinea meant that personal safety was never an issue. My age (32) and awareness of the generalized North American social cues regarding male and female removed me from any potential sexual encounters which might lead to problems concerning personal safety.

Jasperites are, above all, sociable, warm, and friendly. On those encounters where I had no personal introduction, entrance was much easier as a consequence of the generally shared agreement that the recording of the history and development of the region was useful. Recording personal histories became one aspect of this larger goal. The tight information network soon made the researchers known and, in fact, at one point in the research, not to have been interviewed and had your genealogy recorded was taken to be an insult.

The ease of access to information does not mean that there were no suspicions about either the goals of the research or the researchers. Many Jasperites had their own ideas about what we should and should not record. In those cases, it would have been a mistake to have insisted upon our own agenda. It is in this area that the advantage of repeated visits and interviews becomes obvious.

As Rosalie Wax[6] has emphasized, reciprocity is the *sine qua non* for any research situation. It can be extended in a myriad of ways and perhaps the most important exchange I was able to offer was as a nonjudgmental listener. This is not to say that dishes were not washed or potatoes peeled or errands run, only that, in retrospect, to view equality of exchange in the tangible arena of "chores" would be a mistake. Further, there is no question in my mind that the generosity of my Jasperite friends in sharing their thoughts and bits of their lives with an outsider must remain an unbalanced exchange.

The study of one's own society – or a variant of it, with similar language and cultural traditions – has advantages and disadvantages. One is familiar with the language and all its slang variations as well as with the general frames of reference that take the outsider so long to learn.

---

[5] Golde, *op. cit.*, p. 7, suggests that in most field situations women present less threatening images.

[6] R. Wax, "Reciprocity in Fieldwork," in R. H. Adams and J. J. Preiss, eds., *Human Organization Research* (Homewood, Ill.: The Dorsey Press, 1960), pp. 90-98.

However, it is precisely because one is so familiar with many aspects of the culture that field work in one's own society presents hazards.[7]

Field work in an exotic society forces one to examine common everyday behaviours, and although field work in one's "own culture" is enhanced because one does have the base of shared agreement for everyday behaviours, for that precise reason, awareness of the hazards of familiarity is necessary.[8]

Participation in aspects of community life in settings which are commonly taken for granted, such as shopping at the market, checking in at the service station, riding farm machinery, participating in work routines, visiting on the main street of Jasper on Saturday night, or using the telephone, are aspects of common daily behaviours which become important in developing deeper understandings of a particular way of life, and these understandings are crucial for the interpretation of interview material.

There were particular incidents which made explicit some of the substantive problems which are part of everyday life in a sparsely populated agricultural community. The experience of taking care of a host family's livestock for a period of ten days brought home sharply an understanding of the ways in which the needs of the enterprise structure one's time. The experience of struggling with fence gates forced recognition of parents' meaning when they used "gates" as a reason to drive their children to the school bus, or when they said, for example, that they had "four gates to go" to get to school, in order to symbolize the nostalgic hardships of the frontier period. The experience of having a complete stranger (to me) ask if that was my car along a particular road, or at a particular house, at a particular time, brought home the fact that in a small population there is little anonymity.

Close ties were established with particular members of the community with whom I was able to raise "problem" questions for discussion such as, "Since everyone knows everyone else, how do people who break the rules (for example, illegitimacy, adultery) get along?" Furthermore, these friends were able to discuss with me particular anxieties about the research and the researchers in their roles as representatives of the larger system which some felt to be judgmental of rural life.

Questions were raised as to the findings of the research, the "usefulness" of such research and the "point" of it all. Although disagreements remained, nevertheless there was shared agreement that the recording of ways in which people solve common problems could be of "use" to others. In certain groups, these discussions during 1963 and

---

[7] Ernestine Friedl, *Vasilika: A Village in Modern Greece* (New York: Holt, Rinehart and Winston, 1962).

[8] Harold Garfinkle, "Studies of the Routine Grounds of Everyday Activities," *Social Problems,* 2 (1964), 225-250.

1964 antedated many of the same concerns raised among anthropologists regarding the obligations of the researcher.[9] Other questions were raised concerning the problems and solutions of urban living; in raising children, and in relationships between men and women. These discussions filled out the patterns of expectations the community residents held about others.

The study of rural regions in industrial society is more commonly associated with the discipline of rural sociology. And, in fact, in 1963 the interest of anthropologists in industrial countries was minimal. One of the continual questions which we had to deal with was our identification as anthropologists and not as sociologists. Jasperites, familiar with the research of anthropologists in exotic countries, or among "Indians", or as archaeologists, were not quite sure what we were doing in Jasper. They certainly did not regard themselves as unique. (To some degree, this discipline confusion continues today among students and laymen.) Our position then, as now, held that many of the anthropology/sociology discipline distinctions were artificial and not particularly useful for the study of any society — esoteric or familiar.[10] However, the tradition of anthropology which involved long extended periods of field work and which involved interests much wider than social relations, in contrast with the more focused traditions of sociology, set the frame of reference for the conducting of the field work.

The fact that the research was not restricted to a one-shot field session but continued for a period of ten years with more or less continuous contact maintained between the researchers and residents, with visits on both sides, emphasizes the developmental and progressive aspect of the project. The study of family life and its relationship to the agricultural enterprise evolved out of an understanding of the particular pressures upon the individual growing up in that type of setting, an understanding which emerged only after the first field session. In that sense the field work procedure was epigenetic: the next topic investigated was often determined by the answers to the previous questions.

The progressive nature of the research hopefully has reflected an evolving understanding and appreciation of the complexity of factors involved in the social life of Jasper. I hope that this book will make those processes come alive.

---

[9] Dell Hymes, ed., *Reinventing Anthropology* (New York: Random House, 1969).
[10] *Ibid.*, pp. 36-43.

Bibliography

Adams, R. N., *The Second Sowing*. San Francisco: Chandler Publishing Co., 1967.

Adams, R. N., and Preiss, J. J. eds., *Human Organization Research*. Homewood, Ill.: The Dorsey Press, 1960.

Atherton, L., *The Cattle Kings*. Bloomington: Indiana University Press, 1961.

Babchuk, N., and Bates, A. P., "The Primary Relations of Middle Class Couples: A Study of Male Dominance," *American Sociological Review,* 28 (1963), 377-384.

Barkin, David, and Bennett, John W., "Kibbutz and Colony: Collective Economics and the Outside World." *Comparative Studies in Society and History,* 14 (1972), 456-483.

Barnes J. A., "Class and Committees in a Norwegian Island Parish," *Human Relations,* 7 (1954), 39-58.

Bartlett, Richard A., *The New Country*. New York: Oxford University Press, 1974.

Bennett, John W., *Hutterian Brethren: The Agricultural Economy and Social Organization of a Communal People.* Stanford: Stanford University Press, 1967.

―――――, "Microcosm-Macrocosm Relationships in North American Agrarian Society." *American Anthropologist,* 69 (1968), 441-454.

―――――, "Reciprocal Economic Exchanges Among North American Agricultural Operators." *Southwestern Journal of Anthropology,* 24 (1968), 276-309.

―――――, *Northern Plainsmen: Adaptive Strategy and Agrarian Life.* Chicago: Aldine Publishing Co., 1969.

―――――, "Change and Transition in Hutterian Society," in A. W. Rasporich, ed., *Western Canada: Past and Present* (Calgary: McClelland and Stewart, 1975), pp. 120-132.

Bennett, John W., and Kohl, Seena B., "The Social Stratification System of a Post-Frontier Society." Paper presented jointly at the Mid-West Sociological Association Meetings, May 1966.

―――――, "Characterological, Strategic and Institutional Interpretations of Prairie Settlement," in A. W. Rasporich, ed., *Western Canada: Past and Present* (Calgary: McClelland and Stewart West Limited, 1975), pp. 14-27.

Blood, Robert O., *The Family.* New York: The Free Press, 1972.

Bohannon, Paul, "Dyad Dominance and Household Maintenance," in Francis Hsu, ed., *Kinship and Culture* (Chicago: Aldine Publishing Co., 1971) pp. 42-65.

Braroe, Niels W., *Indian & White.* Stanford: Stanford University Press, 1975.

Breimeyer, Harold, *Individual Freedom and the Economic Organization of Agriculture.* Urbana: University of Illinois Press, 1965.

Bronfenbrenner, U., *Two Worlds of Childhood: U.S. and U.S.S.R.* New York: Russell Sage Foundation, 1970.

Census of Canada.

Cumming, Elaine, and Schneider, David, "Sibling Solidarity: A Property of American Kinship," *American Anthropologist,* 63 (1961), 498-507.

Davenport, W., "Introduction," in S. Mintz and W. Davenport, eds., "Working Papers in Caribbean Social Organization," *Social and Economic Studies,* 10 (December 1961, a special number), 380-385.

Eichler, Margrit, "Women as Personal Dependents," in Marylee Stephenson, ed., *Women in Canada* (Toronto: New Press, 1973), 36-55.

Etzioni, Amitai, ed., *Complex Organization: A Social Reader.* New York: Holt, Rinehart and Winston, 1961.

Farber, Bernard, *Family Organization and Interaction.* San Francisco: Chandler Publishing Co., 1964.

Firth, Raymond, Forge, Jane, and Hubert, Anthony, *Families and Their Relations*. London: Humanities Press, 1970.

Fowke, Vernon C., *The National Policy and the Wheat Economy*. Toronto: University of Toronto Press, 1957.

Frankenberg, Ronald, *Communities in Britain*. Harmondsworth, Middx.: Penguin Books Ltd., 1966.

Freilich, Morris, ed., *Marginal Natives: Anthropologists at Work*. New York: Harper and Row, 1970.

Friedl, Ernestine, *Vasilika: A Village in Modern Greece*. New York: Holt, Rinehart and Winston, 1962.

Garfinkle, Harold, "Studies of the Routine Grounds of Everyday Activities." *Social Problems*, 2 (1964), 225-250.

Gibson, J. D., *Family Farm Business Arrangements, Agricultural Economics Bulletin 1*. Manitoba: University of Manitoba, 1959.

Gluckman, Max, "Gossip and Scandal." *Current Anthropology*, 3 (1963), 307-316.

Golde, Peggy, ed., *Women in the Field*. Chicago: Aldine Publishing Co., 1970.

Griswold, Whitney, *Farming and Democracy*. New York: Harcourt Brace and Co., 1948.

Hall, Oswald, and McFarland, Bruce, *Transition from School to Work*. Canadian Department of Labour Report No. 10, 1962.

Hammel, E. A., "The Zadruga as Process," in Peter Laslett, ed., *Household and Family in Past Time* (Cambridge: University Press, 1972), pp. 335-374.

Hess, Robert, and Handel, Gerald, *Family Worlds*. Chicago: University of Chicago Press, 1959.

Hostetler, John A., *Hutterite Society*. Baltimore: The Johns Hopkins University Press, 1974.

Hostetler, John A., and Huntington, Gertrude E., *The Hutterites in North America*. Case Studies in Cultural Anthropology Series. New York: Holt, Rinehart and Winston, 1967.

Hsu, Francis, "A Hypothesis on Kinship and Culture," in Francis Hsu, ed., *Kinship and Culture* (Chicago: Aldine Publishing Co., 1971), pp. 3-29.

Hsu, Francis, ed., *Kinship and Culture*. Chicago: Aldine Publishing Co., 1971.

Humphreys, Alexander J., *New Dubliners: Urbanization and the Irish Family*. New York: Fordham University Press, 1966.

Hymes, Dell, "The Use of Anthropology: Critical, Political, Personal," in Dell Hymes, ed., *Reinventing Anthropology* (New York: Random House, 1969), pp. 4-79.

Hymes, Dell, ed., *Reinventing Anthropology*. New York: Random House, 1969.

Ishwaran, K., ed., *The Canadian Family*. Toronto: Holt, Rinehart and Winston of Canada Ltd., 1971.

Jongmans, D. G., and Gutkind, P. C. W., eds., *Anthropologists in the Field*. New York: Humanities Press, 1967.

Kaplan, Bert, and Plaut, Thomas F. A., *Personality in a Communal Society*. Lawrence; University of Kansas Publications, 1956.

Kohl, Seena B., and Bennett, John W., "Succession to Family Enterprises and the Migration of Young People in a Canadian Agricultural Community," in K. Ishwaran, ed., *The Canadian Family* (Toronto: Holt, Rinehart and Winston of Canada Ltd., 1971), pp. 203-224.

Kohn, M.L., "Social Class and Parent-Child Relationships." *American Journal of Sociology,* 68 (1959), 471-480.

Laslett, Peter, ed., *Household and Family in Past Time*. Cambridge: University Press, 1972.

Lewis, Oscar, "An Anthropological Approach to Family Studies." *American Journal of Sociology*, 55 (1950), 468-475.

Lipman-Blumen, Jean, "Role De-Differentiation as a System Response to Crisis: Occupational and Political Roles of Women." *Sociological Inquiry,* 43 (1973), 105-129.

Lipset, S. M., *Agrarian Socialism*. Garden City, N.J.: Anchor Books, 1968.

Lopata, Helen, *Occupation: Housewife*. Oxford: Oxford University Press, 1971.

Loudon, J. B., "Teasing and Socialization on Tristan da Cunha," in Philip Mayer, ed., *Socialization: The Approach from Social Anthropology* (London: Tavistock Publications , 1970), pp. 293-332.

Lucas, A., ed., *Great Canadian Short Stories*. New York: Dell Publishing Co., 1971.

MacGregor, J. G., *Northwest of Sixteen*. Rutland, Vermont: Charles E. Tuttle Co., 1968.

MacLellan, Margaret E., "History of Women's Rights in Canada," in *Cultural Tradition and Political History of Women in Canada*, Studies of the Royal Commission on the Status of Women in Canada, Report No. 8 (Ottawa: Information Canada, 1971).

Mayer, Philip, ed., *Socialization: The Approach from Social Anthropology*. London: Tavistock Publications, 1970.

Miner, Morace, *Culture and Agriculture: An Anthropological Study of a Corn Belt County.* Ann Arbor, Michigan: Occasional Contributions from the Museum of Anthropology of the University of Michigan, No. 14, 1949.

Mintz, S., and Davenport, W., eds., "Working Papers in Caribbean Social Organization," *Social and Economic Studies,* 10 (December 1961, a special number).

Morris, Audrey Y., *Gentle Pioneers.* Toronto and London: Hodder and Stoughton Ltd., 1971.

Murphy, Yolanda, and Murphy, Robert F., *Women of the Forest.* New York and London: Columbia University Press, 1974.

Neugarten, Bernice L., ed., *Middle Age and Aging.* Chicago: University of Chicago Press, 1968.

Nye, F. Ivan, and Berardo, Felix M., *The Family: Its Structure and Interaction.* New York: The MacMillan Co., 1973.

Ortner, Sherry B., "Is Female to Male as Nature is to Culture?" in M. Z. Rosaldo and L. Lamphere, eds., *Women, Culture and Society* (Stanford: Stanford University Press, 1974), pp. 67-87.

Pearlin, L. I., *Class-context and Family Relations: A Cross-National Study.* Boston: Little, Brown, 1971.

Peters, Victor A., *All Things Common: The Hutterian Way of Life.* Minneapolis: University of Minnesota Press, 1965.

Rabourne, Nellie, "Why There is a Feud Between Ranchers and Farmers." *The Western Producer,* May 28, 1964.

Radcliffe-Brown, A. R., "Introduction," in A. R. Radcliffe-Brown and D. Forde, eds., *African Systems of Kinship and Marriage* (London: Oxford University Press, 1950), pp. 1-85.

Radcliffe-Brown, A. R., and Forde, D.; eds., *African Systems of Kinship and Marriage.* London: Oxford University Press, 1950.

Rasporich, A. W., ed., *Prairie Perspectives 2.* Toronto: Holt, Rinehart and Winston of Canada Ltd., 1974.

_____, *Western Canada: Past and Present.* Calgary: McClelland and Stewart, 1975.

Reiss, Ira L., *The Social Context of Pre-marital Sexual Permissiveness.* New York: Holt, Rinehart and Winston, 1967.

Report of the Royal Commission on the Status of Women in Canada. Ottawa: Information Canada, 1970.

Rosaldo, Michelle Zimbalist, "Women, Culture and Society: A Theoretical Overview," in M. Z. Rosaldo and L. Lamphere, eds., *Women, Culture and Society* (Stanford: Stanford University Press, 1974), pp. 1-42.

Rosaldo, M. Z., and L. Lamphere, eds., *Women, Culture and Society.* Stanford: Stanford University Press, 1974.

Ross, Sinclair, "The Painted Door," in A. Lucas, ed., *Great Canadian Short Stories* (New York: Dell Publishing Co., 1971), pp. 96-115.

Rossi, Alice S., "Equality Between the Sexes: An Immodest Proposal." *Daedalus,* 93 (1964), 607-652.

Rossi, Peter, "The Organizational Structure of An American Community," in Amitai Etzioni, ed., *Complex Organization: A Social Reader* (New York: Holt, Rinehart and Winston, 1961), pp. 301-312.

Rowbotham, Sheila, *Hidden From History.* New York: Random House, 1974.

Schwartz, C., *The Search for Stability: Contemporary Saskatchewan.* Toronto: McClelland and Stewart, 1959.

Seeley, J. R., Sim, R.A., and Loosley, E. W., *Crestwood Heights.* New York: John Wiley and Sons, 1956.

Slater, Philip E., *The Pursuit of Loneliness.* Boston: Beaver Press, 1971.

Smith, Dorothy E., "Women, The Family and Corporate Capitalism," in Marylee Stephenson, ed., *Women in Canada* (Toronto: New Press, 1973), pp. 5-35.

Stegner, Wallace, *Wolf Willow.* New York: The Viking Press, 1955.

Stephenson, Marylee, ed., *Women in Canada.* Toronto: New Press, 1973.

Steward, Julian, *Area Research: Theory and Practice.* Social Science Research Council Bulletin No. 63, 1950.

Straus, Murray A., "Societal Needs and Personal Characteristics in the Choice of Farm, Blue-Collar, and White-Collar Occupations by Farmers' Sons," *Rural Sociology,* 29 (1964), 408-425.

Strong-Boag, Veronica, "Cousin Cinderella: A Guide to Historical Literature Pertaining to Canadian Women" in Marylee Stephenson, ed., *Women in Canada* (Toronto: New Press, 1973), pp. 262-290.

Sussman, Marvin, and Cogswell, B. E., "Interpersonal Competence: An Issue in Cross-National Family Research," in M. B. Sussman and B.E. Cogswell, eds., *Cross-National Family Research* (Leiden: E. J. Brill, 1972), pp. 205-222.

Sussman, M. B., and Cogswell, B. E., eds., *Cross-National Family Research.* Leiden: E. J. Brill, 1972.

Sweester, D., "The Structure of Sibling Relationships." *American Journal of Sociology,* 76 (1970), 47-58.

Talmon, Yonina, "Aging in Israel, A Planned Society," in Bernice Neugarten, ed., *Middle Age and Aging* (Chicago: University of Chicago Press, 1968), pp. 461-468.

Townsend, Peter, *The Family Life of Old People.* New York: The Free Press of Glencoe, 1957.

Wakil, S. Parvez. "Campus Mate Selection Preferences: A Cross-National Comparison." *Social Forces,* 51 (1973), 471-476.

Wax, Rosalie, "Reciprocity in Fieldwork," in R. N. Adams and J. J. Preiss, eds., *Human Organization Research* (Homewood, Ill.: The Dorsey Press, 1960), pp. 90-98.

———, *Doing Fieldwork: Warnings and Advice.* Chicago: University of Chicago Press, 1971.

Young, Michael, and Willmott, Peter, *Family and Kinship in East London.* Glencoe: The Free Press, 1957.